COWGIRL UP!

A History of Rodeoing Women

HEIDI M. THOMAS

TWODOT®

GUILFORD, CONNECTICUT
HELENA, MONTANA

A · TWODOT® · BOOK

Copyright © 2014 by Heidi M. Thomas

TwoDot is a registered trademark of Morris Book Publishing, LLC.

Project Editor: Staci Zacharski
Layout Artist: Melissa Evarts

Library of Congress Cataloging-in-Publication data is available on file.

ISBN 978-0-7627-8964-1

Printed in the United States of America

*To the Montana cowgirls who made history
during the Golden Age of rodeo*

Contents

Acknowledgments

Thank you to my beta readers, Sharon Anderson and Sally Harper Bates, and to all of my writer friends for encouraging me through the years—you know who you are! Thank you to my husband and my family for your support. And thank you to Erin Turner, Staci Zacharski, and Katie Sharp at Globe Pequot/TwoDot Press for your confidence in publishing my work and working with me to make it better.

PREFACE

HOME GROWN FROM THE EVERYDAY WORLD OF CATTLE RANCHING, rodeo's roots and many terms stem from the Spanish conquistadors of the 1700s. The first rodeos began in the mid-1800s with informal contests held among working cowboys (a translation of the Spanish word *vaquero*) to see who could ride the meanest bronc or rope a steer the fastest. A hundred years ago bronc busting didn't have the lifesaving luxury of a buzzer going off after eight seconds. Cowboys rode until they were bucked off or the horse gave up, whichever came first. Some of those rides lasted up to twenty minutes.

Events later became more organized when cowboys drove thousands of cattle and horses to town in the yearly roundup, usually around July 4th. At the end of these long trail drives, the cowhands would celebrate by competing to see who was the best bronc rider, roper, or steer wrestler. With the advent of cross-country railroads, these trail drives faded away, but Wild West shows began to crop up, and cowboys continued to demonstrate their prowess at paid entertainment events. Montana joined the ranks of states holding commercial rodeos in 1896.

The first cowgirls learned to ride out of necessity to help on their family ranches. At an early age they learned to ride horses, rope cattle, and stay in the saddle atop an untamed bucking bronco. They competed with men in those early ranch gatherings and continued to do so at the organized roundup events.

In 1885 Annie Oakley, a diminutive sharpshooter in Buffalo Bill Cody's Wild West Show, paved the way for other women to be recognized in the Wild West show arena. Two years later Bertha Kaepernick (Blancett) was allowed to enter a horse race in Cheyenne's Frontier Days. But the arena was so muddy the cowboys refused to participate. To entertain the crowd, she was coerced into riding a bucking horse. Despite the terrible conditions, she managed to stay in the saddle and put the men to shame. She continued to compete and often beat such legendary cowboys as Ben Corbett and Hoot Gibson.

A publicist for a Wild West show once said, "Rodeos will never replace Wild West shows for one good reason—they don't have beautiful cowgirls." Women have continued to prove him wrong to this day.

The term "cow girl" had been around for many years but became one word when the national *Police Gazette* printed it as such in 1893, and Montgomery Ward also put the two words together in 1895. Although the word was already in use, Lucille Mulhall of Oklahoma is popularly known as the "first cowgirl." One story has Teddy Roosevelt dubbing her with the title after witnessing her ride at the family ranch, and another story states it was Will Rogers who gave her the name. Lucille was among the first women to compete in roping and riding events against men and earned the title "Champion Lady Steer Roper of the World."

Some women today don't like the word *cowgirl*, but as a writer in *Texas Monthly* magazine stated in 1987, the word is not necessarily derogatory. "Like it or not, the word calls up a range of resonant images: the coquettish trick rider in a Wild West show; the self-reliant ranch woman who brands and doctors her own calves; the suburban mother who spends every night and weekend running barrels; the bull rider who drives hundreds of miles to an All-Girl rodeo, hoping to win maybe a couple hundred dollars."

Cowgirl is a state of mind, to paraphrase Dale Evans, who goes on to say, "Cowgirl is a pioneer spirit, a special American brand of courage. The cowgirl faces life head on, lives by her own lights, and makes no excuses. Cowgirls take stands. They speak up. They defend the things they hold dear. A cowgirl might be a rancher, or a barrel racer, or a bull rider, or an actress. But she's just as likely to be a checker at the local Winn Dixie, a full-time mother, a banker, an attorney, or an astronaut."

World War I nearly killed rodeo, but the sport rose from the ashes and grew to greater prominence, not in the West where it was born but in the big cities of the East. Until 1922, cowboys and cowgirls who won at Cheyenne Frontier Days, which began in 1897, were considered the world's champions. Tex Austin created the Madison Square Garden Rodeo in 1922, which immediately became the premier national event. Madison Garden winners were thereafter recognized as the unofficial world champions, including several Montana cowgirls.

When Austin lost control of the Madison Square Garden contest, Col. William T. Johnson from Texas took over the Garden rodeo. He soon began producing rodeos in other Eastern indoor arenas, including Boston.

By 1920 rodeos regularly featured three cowgirl events—ladies' bronc riding, trick riding, and, at rodeos with a race track, cowgirls' relay racing. To score in the saddle bronc event, women had to stay on board eight seconds (the men rode ten) and they were allowed to ride with two reins, although they could opt to use one as the men did. Women were often required to ride with hobbled stirrups (stirrups held fast by a strap underneath the horse, supposedly to prevent them from falling off). The time limit changed to eight seconds for men and six seconds for women during the 1950s.

Although the rodeo world has probably heard more about national female riders like Lucille Mulhall, Prairie Rose Henderson, and Tad Lucas, Montana's cowgirls ranked right up there with the best. Fannie Sperry, born in 1887, led the way in women's rodeo when she rode her first bronc at age fourteen.

Montana, where rodeos grew out of the rolling prairie of Big Sky Country, provides some of the West's richest rodeo heritage and some of the most famous women riders.

Montana cowgirls were intrepid, hardworking, and courageous. They defined the modern term "cowgirl up," an expression that means to rise to the occasion, not to give up, and to do it all without whining or complaining. It is easy to say "cowgirl up"; however, it takes a true cowgirl at heart to live up to the true meaning.

This is the story of Montana's courageous women of rodeo.

CHAPTER ONE

Rodeo Is No Place for Women

"Ruins the events for us men"

Dust filled the air, giving the clear blue sky a brownish haze. Steers bawled in their pens, broncs kicked their stalls, and the rodeo announcer bellowed out the name of the next rider.

A baby let out a lusty yell. Margie Greenough Henson turned to the wooden apple box, where her son lay on a pillow, and picked him up, clucking and shushing.

Her sister, Alice, called from the chutes, "You're up next, and I'm after you."

The slender red-haired Margie waved her acknowledgment and turned to a lanky cowboy standing nearby. "Here, would you hold Chuck for me while I ride? It's only for eight seconds."

The Greenough sisters, who are listed in both the National Cowgirl Hall of Fame and the National Cowboy Hall of Fame, epitomized the Montana cowgirls of the early 1900s and bridged the final transition between the Old West and the modern era.

A woman bronc rider earned her living by beating competitors (often men), wearing men's clothing, and living around cowboys. She had to be tough; otherwise she'd have been squeezed out. Home was on the plains and on the road, with little room for fluff. But this life didn't necessarily make her "hard-boiled."

Marie Gibson on bronc, Ski-Hi Stampede COURTESY OF ANN MARIE STAMEY

Montana's Greenough sisters, Fannie Sperry Steele, Marie Gibson, Bobby Brooks Kramer, Jane Burnett Smith, the Brander sisters, trick riders Birdie Askin and Trixi McCormick, and pickup rider Ann Secrest Hanson proved that athleticism and femininity are not mutually exclusive.

The *London Evening News* validated these accomplishments in its report of the cowgirls in the Tex Austin Wild West Troupe in 1924: "It is amazing to see these slips of girls take fearful tosses while fighting outlaw horses, and then half an hour later it is still more amazing to see these same girls strolling out to tea in their Parisian frocks."

The following quote about Lucille Mulhall of Oklahoma in a 1900 *New York World* article could also have described most of these Montana women: ". . . only ninety pounds, can break a bronc, lasso and brand a steer, and shoot a coyote at 500 yards. She can also play Chopin, quote Browning, and make mayonnaise."

In the late 1800s and early 1900s the public image of rodeo cow-girls was as "loose women" because they participated in a tough, dangerous men's occupation; traveled around the country with men; and often wore men's clothing. They were generally not thought of as wives and mothers, and rodeo riding was considered detrimental to women's reproductive organs, but most of them did have children, like Margie Greenough Henson. In fact she told the *Arizona Daily Star* in a 1994 interview, "In the fall of 1930, I was riding bucking broncs and he [her son, Chuck] was born in February of '31."

Margie's sister, Alice, was quoted in *Physical Culture* magazine in 1937:

> *A cow-woman takes no coddling, gets no martyr complex just because she is going to have a baby. She rides in the show up until two months before she expects the child—and she is back in the saddle, bronc-riding in contest not later than six weeks afterward. This is the reward of developing strong backs, erect posture, educated muscles.*
>
> *Women with curved spines and swayed abdomens, with half the muscles in their bodies wasted from lack of exercise and use, who fear childbirth because they have not kept their bodies natural, wonder why their lives are not rich, full, vital—yet they never dream that the violation of natural health law is the cause of everything.*

Even Annie Oakley said, "I think sport and healthful exercise makes women better, healthier and happier."

Marie Gibson of Havre, mother of three children and a world champion bronc rider, also helped disprove the widespread belief that athletic women were incapable of childbearing and unsuitable for marriage.

This idea of the danger of riding to femininity had its roots in feudal times when royal families, in an effort to offset the accidental loss of virginity, prohibited aristocratic girls from riding astride.

The nineteenth-century medical profession also warned that if women "unduly exerted themselves," they would be more likely than men to suffer nervous exhaustion, known as "neurasthenic disease." They held the belief that too much exercise could harm female participants, physically and psychologically, and detract from or even diminish their femininity. Physicians counseled young women to curtail their physical and even intellectual activity during their menstrual periods, and gave medical advice such as, "Long walks are to be avoided . . . all severe physical exertion . . . intense mental excitement, such as a fit of anger or grief or even intense joy may be injurious."

And still in 1912 *Harper's Bazaar,* a popular American magazine for women, posed an ominous question about exercise and fertility with its article titled "Are Athletics a Menace to Motherhood?" Nearly seventy-five years later, an article in the same women's magazine continued to wonder, "Can Sports Make You Sterile?"

Even physical education instructors in the late 1890s strongly opposed competition among women, fearing it would make them less feminine. And women rodeo riders faced the same social stigma well into the 1900s.

Montana women knew innately that if they were strong enough and good enough to do men's work, they could certainly compete with them. Ben Greenough of Red Lodge (who earned the first recorded Montana bronc riding title in 1898) gathered wild horses, broke them, and sold them. He would point out several unbroken mounts, saying, "Well, Frank, take this. Alice, you take that. And Marge, take that one." His mantra to his eight children (including his daughters) was, "If you can't ride 'em, walk." And they did. "We didn't walk very often," Alice quipped. It was said Ben knew that by the time those wild horses got tired of trying to dislodge his tenacious daughters, they would be tame enough for the average person to ride.

Alice and Margie began riding in rodeos in 1929 with their brothers Bill and Turk as the "Riding Greenoughs."

Fannie Sperry (Steele) was practically born on the back of a horse. Her mother rode with her babies perched in front of her on the saddle.

Fannie helped her mother and brother take care of their ranch in the Beartooth Mountains when her father became disabled. A consummate horse lover, she began her career at a neighborhood rodeo in 1901 at age fourteen, when she rode a wild bronc she had captured herself.

Fannie went on to become a record holder in the relay race, Montana Lady Bucking Horse Champion in 1907, and Lady Bucking Horse Champion of the World at the first Calgary Stampede in 1912. But she and the other Montana cowgirls heard remarks such as, "Most ladies I know wear dresses." "If you ask me, they oughtta keep those fool women out of exhibition. A female ain't got no business on a bucking horse." "Ruins the event for us men." "Women are built for havin' babies, not riding broncs."

Just after hearing the thrilling words, "Ladies and gentlemen, the Lady Bucking Horse Champion of Montana—Fannieeee . . . Sperry!" and the roar of the crowd, spectators surged onto the field to congratulate her. But Fannie was also painfully aware of a group of women passing by with disdainful looks and she overheard, "What kind of a lady would make such a spectacle of herself?"

One newspaper article reiterated the Victorian belief that "Horseback riding is physically unhygienic for women, except when the sidesaddle is employed." Fannie and her friends just laughed.

Even Fannie's own mother worried about her daughter's reputation, telling her after her debut bronc ride, "I heard some rude remarks when you climbed onto that bronco. Riding and breaking horses for the ranch is one thing. A public display is another. Besides, it's too risky."

Later, after Fannie had convinced her mother to allow her to participate in relay races, Mrs. Sperry still had reservations: "I know horses ain't the only fast things at them races." And when Fannie wanted to attend the Calgary Stampede, her dad was reluctant to let her go, saying, "It isn't proper for a twenty-five-year-old woman to be parading herself like that. You should be thinking about settling down."

Cowgirls were also criticized for the clothing they wore. *Practical Etiquette*, published in 1899, stated "It is very bad taste, even for a frolic, for a young woman to assume boys' clothes, or get herself up in any way that will tend to make herself look masculine."

A study published by *The Female Offender* in 1895 posited that "women who looked and acted like males were probably congenital criminals."

And, according to the *New York Times* in May 1867, "any women who thirst[ed] for trousers was mentally ill, the victim of a curious mental disorder that involved hysteria and hallucinations."

Even in the early 1940s, bronc rider Jane Burnett Smith encountered criticism when she arrived at Madison Square Garden. Riding in an elevator, one woman remarked to another, "Look at what she's wearing. How can they walk with those things on their feet?"

"And those tight pants," the other woman added. "Imagine going out in public dressed like that."

Annie Oakley was the most famous Old West personality and the forerunner of the rodeo cowgirl. She toured with Buffalo Bill for seventeen years as an expert marksman. All this while wearing dresses.

But while working their ranches, women discovered that riding astride—as Native American women had done since the mid-seventeenth century—was much more practical and comfortable, less tiring and dangerous than sidesaddle, and cowgirls who rode astride gained a slow acceptance.

The December 1906 *Ladies Home Journal* stated, "Many young girls are now taught to ride cross-saddle, as the old style of sidesaddle is thought to make a girl become crooked."

Necessity being the mother of invention, and since most women were handy at sewing, they began to remodel their long skirts into the split riding skirt. Even with that adaptation, the skirts were still long, voluminous, and cumbersome. But that didn't seem to cramp the cowgirls' style. They rode bucking broncs and bulls and roped and tied steers, often beating their male counterparts.

Margie Greenough, Dorothy Dollerhide, Nancy Shepard, Fay Blackstone (all the ladies designed and made their outfits) FROM MARGIE GREENOUGH COLLECTION, COURTESY OF LEIGH ANN BILLINGSLEY

Despite these accomplishments, this progressive fashion was frowned upon, as Evelyn Cameron found out in 1895. The English photographer, turned Montana rancher, cantered into Miles City one fine August day, wearing a split riding skirt she had made herself. While doing her shopping, she was suddenly confronted by a group of outraged townswomen, backed by the sheriff, who threatened her with arrest if she didn't leave town.

"After riding into town forty-eight miles from the ranch, I was much amused at the laughing and giggling girls who stood staring at my costume as I walked about," she wrote later.

Cowgirls were not to be thwarted, however. They had discovered this fashion as a riding tool. The newspaper in Havre, Montana, August 1897, reported:

> There were six young women who competed in the bronc riding competition. The broncos chosen were as villainous a crew of ponies as ever got together. The riders wore a combination costume of cowboy and bicycler's wardrobes. There was no pretense about sidesaddles as all the broncos were ridden astraddle. The mix-ups were so lively that it seemed the riders would be reduced to their high heeled boots. Sombreros and whips were lost, the riders' long hair whipped in the wind, and their clothes had the appearance of having been used as street sweepers. But there were no serious rents in garments and not even a scratch on any pretty face.

One of Fannie Sperry's teammates on the relay team sported a new costume on a tour stop in Denver in 1906—full calf-length "bloomers," gathered above her boots and topped with a matching short top. This style had been introduced by the flamboyant Prairie Rose Henderson of Wyoming, who created quite a stir with this "racy" look.

While Fannie's first response was "Where's your skirt?" she and her friends decided this costume looked very practical, so they had black bloomers made for the team. They created their own stir when they debuted in Grand Rapids, Michigan. They were greeted with gasps and tittering, then whistles and hoots, from the grandstand. But this response did not deter them; they continued to wear their new comfortable, practical outfits.

Other cowgirls found similar comfortable costumes for rodeo riding. Marie Gibson was shown in photos wearing split skirts, jodhpurs, or slacks. Each cowgirl dressed distinctively, many wearing calf-length split skirts made of leather and embellished with fringe, beads, or brass studs. Colorful satin shirts, bright silk scarves, and tall wide-brimmed hats added to the costume.

Fannie Sperry and the "Montana Girls" show off their bloomer costumes. COURTESY OF VIOLA HILGER NELSON

Around 1925 Vera McGinnis (California, 1892–1990) became the first cowgirl to wear pants in the arena. Considering skirts and tight breeches as nuisances, McGinnis created a pair of trousers from a pair of boys' flannel pants with a zipper on the side. She remarked, "I like to wear them so then I can kick up my heels as I like."

Cowgirls felt they belonged in the saddle and loved the open prairie, horses, guns, and competition, but most still loved dressing up and showing their feminine side. A woman could be tough and competitive, but in public she should definitely look like a girl.

The Greenough sisters were talented seamstresses as well as riders and carried a sewing machine along on the road. Not liking the short pants that ended below the knee when they were starting out, "we bought a pair of sailor pants, took them apart and made a pattern," Margie later told the *Arizona Daily Star*. From then on they designed and sewed their own bell-bottomed trousers and bolero jackets.

"Each cowgirl was an individual who dressed in her own style. Most designed their own clothes and tailored them to fit neatly and well," Alice wrote in a 1974 article titled "Cowgirls of Yesterday" in *Persimmon Hill* magazine. "I can remember when a cowboy was required to wear dress pants in the Grand Entry in New York and Boston; if he was wearing Levis he had to wear chaps over them. A cowgirl in Levis during a performance was unheard of, unthinkable."

Alice also expressed her opinion in a 1937 article in *Physical Culture* magazine: "A cowgirl would no more think of wearing spike heels, a tight girdle, a binding brassiere, than she would drink poison. It is not that a cowgirl does not want to attract the masculine eyes, but we know cowboys. They like slimness, line, grace—but they want it natural."

Alice and Margie enjoyed shopping for new fabrics in New York after rodeo events to sew their rodeo clothes, but they soon decided not to wear Western clothing while out in the "Big Apple," since crowds followed them around town, enamored with the attractive costumes they designed.

Nothing seemed to daunt these intrepid cowgirls, not clothing restrictions nor children, not society's gasps nor men's opposition. When a group of cowboys attempted to get up a petition to have women thrown out of the Pendleton Roundup in 1910, complaining that "girls spoil the horses and water down the events till there's no challenge," Fannie Sperry scoffed, "You're wrong, mister. Just watch us."

And the world did. Fannie, Marie, Bobby, Jane, and the Greenough and Brander sisters proved everyone wrong. They had the passion, the courage, and the dream, and nothing was going to stand in their way.

CHAPTER TWO

Motivation to Compete

"Believe you can and you're halfway there."
—TEDDY ROOSEVELT

The wind howled outside the ranch house at Gilt Edge, Montana, one morning just a few days before Jane Burnett's seventh birthday in 1926. She scraped a small peephole through the frost on the window. Nothing was visible—no livestock in the corral or around the feed racks—nothing but drifting snow. Jane shivered and turned back to eating breakfast.

Visions of eating popcorn and stretching out on the calf-hide rug near the potbellied coal stove in the living room were quickly squelched when Grandpa Bill rose from the table. "Clinton, you'd better pick up those colts today. They're with Hedman's horses."

Jane's dad, Clinton, turned to her. "Well? Wanna go along?" It was not really a question, and there was only one acceptable reply.

"Sure," she said. The subzero weather seemed a minor issue compared to the idea of being considered unable to "take it."

Jane's Shetland pony jogged along beside her daddy's horse, nearly high centering in many of the deeper drifts. Time froze, along with her limbs. When they found the horses in a set of abandoned corrals, her father indicated with a nod of his head that she was to wait near the entrance in case the animals tried to get away.

Several diminishing degrees later, she was still sitting hunched over the saddle horn, teeth chattering and icicles hanging from the end of her nose.

Finally her daddy rode up to her. He never questioned whether she was frozen, if she was all right, or how she felt. He simply asked matter-of-factly, "You hired out as a tough hand, didn't you?"

Nothing else was necessary.

In the years to come, this incident would serve as a foundation for Jane's life. Later she said, "My early childhood made me stronger, more independent."

She rode her first steer for fifty cents at age eleven. At twelve, she sneaked away from the ranch on many weekends and hitchhiked to any rodeo within an area of three hundred to four hundred miles, where she rode steers for "mount money."

Jane continued her journey for the next twenty years in one-chute, small-town rodeos from the Canadian border to Mexico City, Los Angeles to Madison Square Garden in New York. She worked for Gene Autry, riding broncs in rodeos he promoted and working as an extra or stunt woman in several Western movies. During her career Jane experienced not only the best of the sport—the rodeo people who were closer than her real family—but she also had to fight the dark side of early day rodeo—unscrupulous promoters, leering drunks, and abusive relationships.

Jane Burnett Smith wrote in her memoir, *Hobbled Stirrups*, "All because I had hired out for a tough hand and thought I had to follow through without complaining. I asked for no sympathy and gave no excuses."

In her book's introduction Jane wrote,

From the scared kid riding his first steer, to the crippled old saddle bronc rider who is going to try it just one more season, each individual secretly believes himself capable of developing into one of the "greats." Without this belief there would be no competition.

Jane Burnett Smith with Gene Autry COURTESY OF CAMILLE SMITH

I consider myself a charter member of these forever hopefuls who doggedly struggled in the shadows of the champions. During my rodeo years I . . . never at any time doubted that I would eventually hold the title of World's Champion Woman Bronc Rider.

However, she wrote, "It seems I was the only person who was genuinely surprised when this failed to occur."

At one point Jane expressed her intention to quit rodeoing to a group of cowboys, who broke into laughter as if she'd just told the biggest joke of the season. "Did I say something funny?" Jane asked.

"You sure did," one replied. "In case nobody ever told you, it's as tough to quit this business as it would be to get off of whiskey, cigarettes, or dope. We've all tried to stop rodeoing—at least once a year—an' the first thing you know, we're right back in there."

That passion, the hunger for the burst of adrenaline, the thrill of the victory echoed by the cheers of the crowd, is something cowgirls find difficult to explain. Fannie Sperry Steele said, "How can I explain to dainty delicate women what it's like to climb down into a rodeo chute onto the back of a wild horse? How can I tell them it is a challenge that lies deep in the bones—a challenge that may go back to prehistoric man and his desire to conquer the outlaw and the wilderness."

The history of the cowgirl shows the sense of freedom they were able to experience, not hobbled by the restraints of social convention. They felt alive with a good horse under them, the wind blowing through their hair, the exhilaration of a fast ride or conquering a thousand-pound bucking animal. All these Montana cowgirls began at an early age, working alongside their fathers, brothers, and husbands, and learned to ride as well as the men, so why not experience the same thrill in the rodeo arena?

❦

Antoinette Marie Gibson, also known as "Buckskin Mary" or "Ma" Gibson, was born near Winnipeg, Canada, on August 18, 1894, and named for the famous queen. A "tomboy," Marie learned to love horses at an early age. She had a black pony and helped on her Belgium-born father's farm, learning the ways of ranching and handling horses and cattle. Later she helped gentle horses as saddle mounts for her father's female customers at his livery stable in Saskatchewan. Her father also owned several racehorses, and while still a teen Marie became one of the few licensed women jockeys in North America.

The love of animals, coupled with early responsibilities, an independent spirit, and bravery, would be a major influence on her future life.

At age fifteen Marie married a neighbor boy, Joseph Dumont, and had four children. One child died at three months, and later her daughter Lucy drowned at age nineteen. How she must have grieved over her losses, which most likely helped her find an inner strength to accomplish what she did.

In 1914 the Dumonts moved to Montana in a covered wagon, where her parents had already moved. They homesteaded at Burnham, ten miles west of Havre, a town that no longer exists.

The marriage failed, and Marie was forced to become the sole support of her children. She became friends with neighbor "Long" George Francis, a local rodeo rider who gave her the nickname "Buckskin Mary" (which she didn't care for), and his friends Ray Ellis (who had introduced bulldogging to the Havre area), Jack Maybee, and Clayton Jolley. Marie watched them break wild horses to use for saddle and team animals, and soon, with their encouragement, she began riding bucking broncs, not always successfully.

At one rodeo her bronc stumbled and she ended up on its neck. The rodeo manager joked that she had bronc riding confused with bull dogging. Other women riders laughed at her clumsy efforts. Marie told one cowgirl, "When I have been riding as much as you have, I'll do better."

Foghorn Clancy, a famous announcer, program man, and rodeo publicist (much of that time at Madison Square Garden), wrote of Marie Gibson in his book *My 50 Years in Rodeo:*

[At the Medicine Hat Stampede in Alberta, Canada] . . . I met for the first time, a girl who was later to become the world's champion

cowgirl bronc rider. . . . Her name on the program was Mary Dumont—a name under which she achieved no great reputation, for she was bucked off the first horse she tried to ride. She came back the next day and rode again. She was "popped" considerably, as she hadn't yet learned the knack of keeping her neck stiff to support her head. . . . On this ride she stayed to the finish.

After the second ride she came up to me. "Foghorn," she said, "what do you think of my chances in the bronc-riding game?"

"Well," I answered, "you certainly have one of the chief require-ments and that is plenty of nerve. If you keep on riding and keep on living, you ought to be able to make the grade. You might even become a champion. Who knows?"

As you can see, I wasn't overenthusiastic. And judging from this first performance of hers I had no idea that she was really to become famous and be a champion. Under the name of Marie "Ma" Gibson, she rode at the biggest rodeos in the United States, from California to Madison Square Garden and was nearly always in the winning column. At one time or another during her long career in the arena, she won over nearly every other cowgirl bronc rider of her time.

Marie's successful rodeo career began with her debut at Havre's 1917 Francis- and Maybee-produced Great Northern Stampede, where she won third money in the horseracing event. This rodeo was also one of Fannie Sperry's major appearances. The Montana cowgirls were truly one big rodeo "family," often meeting and competing at events all over the country.

That summer Marie also met her future husband, Tom Gibson, a professional bronc rider from Canada who had won the 1914 amateur championship of the provinces. They were married in 1918, and she acquired the last name she would make famous.

After that first rodeo in Havre, Marie plunged into the rodeo cir-cuit, riding in Canadian rodeos at Nelson, Medicine Hat, Calgary, Moose Jaw, Regina, and stops in between.

In September 1919 Marie received a huge boost to her career at the Saskatoon rodeo, where she won the Best Woman Bronc Rider award.

"Competition was keen and there was a great deal of rivalry between the girls and the men." Marie later related her experience. "The Prince (Edward) of Wales sat in the grandstand in the royal pavilion draped with flags and streamers. . . . I drew Sugar Company. He was a big horse with a mean look in his eye. He bucked right out in front of the royal pavilion and sure came undone. Being a great big horse and I weighing only 96 pounds, I stayed with him, but it was all I could do."

When she'd finished her ride, Marie received a big hand of applause and was summoned before the prince. "The prince, he is a handsome one, and quite the ladies' man. . . . I was ashamed to go to the stand all dusty from riding and the wind blowing, but he congratulated me on my ride and said he would like to live out west with us."

She asked him if he'd like to ride, and he was quite enthusiastic about the idea. So she had one of the trick horses brought out, and he rode back and forth in front of the grandstand. The prince also donned a wide-brimmed hat and posed for pictures in front of the crowd.

After the rodeo was over, Mayor McMillan presented Marie with a diamond pendant and a gold vanity case that he said had been left by the prince for the best lady bronc rider.

While at this rodeo, another cowgirl dared her to ride a Brahma steer, saying she would ride one if Marie did. Well, her husband, Tom, had told her earlier that those huge animals were too dangerous and she wasn't to be riding one, so she said no.

The promoter laughed at her. "I never knew you to be a coward, Marie."

She answered, "I've never ridden a steer and have no right to try."

"I know what's the matter with you, you're getting cold feet," he taunted.

The five-foot, ninety-six-pound Marie didn't like the idea of being called a coward. "Just put a surcingle on one, and I'll show you I'm not afraid, even if he throws me."

Marie Gibson and the Prince of Wales in Saskatoon COURTESY OF ANN MARIE STAMEY

The other cowgirl came out of the chute first and rode about four jumps before she hit the dirt, knocked out cold. "We carried her out of the arena and then my name was announced," Marie wrote later. She thought maybe being "yellow" wasn't so bad after all but had no time to back out before she was on the big black steer's back and he was bursting through the chute.

"About the second or third jump he kicked both my spurs off," Marie related. "I went reaching for him but he was not to be found, so I hit the dirt, and he jumped over me." The crowd hushed, but she got up, unhurt.

This experience gave her confidence, and she continued to ride steers from then on, as well as broncs and exhibiting trick riding. (Steers in those days were wild off the prairie and much larger than the ones the kids ride in rodeos today, and they were also often included in the men's events.) Marie and Tom rode the circuit together for several years, until he was injured and stayed home to work their ranch and small coal mine a few miles west of Havre.

———

Fannie Sperry Steele, born March 27, 1887, learned to ride on the family ranch near Helena almost as soon as she could walk. When she was two years old, she told her horse-loving mother, "I'm gonna catch me a white-faced horsie." Pintos were always her favorites, and by age six she had her own horse.

She later wrote, "If there is a horse in the zodiac then I am sure I must have been born under its sign, for the horse has shaped and determined my whole way of life."

Although she preferred working with horses to going to school, the daily event that kept her enthusiastic was racing to the schoolhouse on horseback with her neighbor and best friend, Christine Synness.

Fannie had more than an average knack with horses, and neighbors often watched her break horses in the Sperry corral, commenting with surprise on her skills. One admirer once observed that Fannie must have been born with glue on the seat of her pants.

At fourteen Fannie caught her own wild stallion and became an expert at gentling and breaking horses. That same year at the Mitchell Fourth of July rodeo, she heard an announcement that the producers were short on riders and would pay five dollars to anyone who would sign up to ride a bucking horse.

Eager for a chance to earn some money, Fannie approached the man in charge. "Mr. Hager, I'd like to sign up for the contest."

He tried to brush her off, pointing toward the schoolhouse where the "women's exhibit" was. Fannie persisted. "I can ride." She turned to Christine's father, Andreas Synness. "Tell him it's all right."

Synness came to her rescue, telling the organizer that she was "a heck of a rider. I don't see any harm in letting her ride. I can vouch for her, I've seen her ride some pretty tough broncs up at my place."

Hager finally relented and allowed her to enter.

Fannie drew a bay named Spitfire, borrowed a hat, and accepted a boost into the saddle. Bucking and whirling, stretching skyward, then jerking his head down toward the ground, the bronc tried his best to unseat the young girl, but she stayed on him until he tired, finishing in second place.

"Good goin', Fannie! Nice ride! You rode 'im like a champion," came praise from the cowboys. At the dance that evening, she was surrounded by young men, eager to talk about her ride. The adrenaline, the attention and accolades, plus knowing she could ride as well as any man, fueled Fannie's lifelong obsession with horses and competition.

In her later years Fannie wrote,

Perhaps it is odd that a woman should be born with an all-consuming love of horseflesh, but I have never thought so. It seems to me as normal as breathing air or drinking water . . . If there are not horses in heaven, I do not want to go there . . .

I can truthfully say that if I had it all to do over again, I would live it exactly the same. From such a statement you gather that I have liked it. I have loved it, every single, wonderful, suffering, exhilarating, damned, blessed moment of it. And if, with my present arthritis, I must pay the price of every bronco ride that

*I have ever made, then I pay for it gladly. Pain is not too great
a price to pay for the freedom of the saddle and a horse between
the legs.*

Alice Greenough would concur. As a little girl, Alice met Fannie, and the two-time Women's Bucking Horse Champion of the World in 1912 and 1913 would serve as her role model. Despite more broken bones than the average person can count, Alice's love of the rodeo game kept her riding, from her first rodeo bronc at age seventeen to exhibition bronc riding at age fifty-seven in 1959.

In 1919 a group of cowboys dared Alice to ride a bucking horse at a rodeo in Forsyth, Montana. "They brought over a gray bronc and saddled him and turned me loose in front of the grandstand," Greenough wrote. "I didn't buck off."

And that began her lifelong wild ride that would take her to rodeos in New York's Madison Square Garden and Boston Garden to Europe, Australia, and Spain.

After the failure of her marriage to Ray Cahill, which produced two children, Alice was working in a rooming house in 1929. She and her sister, Margie, saw an ad in *Billboard* magazine: "Cowgirls Wanted" for Jack King's Wild West Show. They packed their clothes and then went to tell their parents.

Although their mother was shocked and dismayed, their dad, Ben "Packsaddle" Greenough, said, "You always did have more guts than good sense anyway, so go on. Just take Old Willy with you." That was his name for willpower.

And so they did. When the train chugged through Red Lodge, the sisters climbed aboard. "We were the only two women, except for Jack's wife," Margie said. They started out living in a tent and being paid fourteen dollars a week. The sisters became well known in rodeo circles all over the country, riding as a team or individually in races, competing on bucking broncs and in exhibitions for trick riding.

＿ ⚫ ＿

Fannie Sperry Steele mentored two more Montana cowgirls, Violet and Margaret Brander of Avon. She gave them jobs on her ranch when they were seventeen and eighteen, respectively, after they had a spat with their father and left home.

"Fannie was a real horsewoman. She was no fake," Marg said later in the documentary *I'll Ride That Horse*. "She was my hero. I'd watch her to see how she did it."

Shortly after their high school graduation, they met famous Montana cowboy Paddy Ryan, who asked Vi to ride double on a steer with him. After that Vi and Marg became well known on the Western rodeo circuit, not only for their bronc riding skills but also for their exhibition double rides on Brahma steers. Marg sat on the neck backward, and Vi rode facing her sister.

"Anything a cowboy can do, we can do better" was their motto. That was motivation enough for Montana cowgirls.

CHAPTER THREE

The 1920s: Heyday for Cowgirls

*"Courage is being scared to death but
saddling up anyway!"*

—JOHN WAYNE

The 1920s are known as the "heyday" of women's rodeo, producing more world champion female riders than any time since. Montana's cowgirls were products of working-ranch values, where athleticism, skill, competitiveness, and grit were acceptable traits in women. Some cowboys, such as Mr. Hager in Fannie Sperry's case, were skeptical of women rodeo riders, and society in general branded them "loose women."

But these cowgirls proved themselves capable of surviving the rough life of rodeo, while still hanging on to their femininity, and they became accomplished athletes well ahead of the athletic and feminist movement of the 1970s.

According to the article "The Stampede" in the Thursday, January 31, 1929, edition of the *New York Times*:

> *Rearing, bucking, fighting, a frenzied bronco tears at the burden on its back. Claimed by a thousand devils, he kicks and plunges with*

1927

Marie Gibson

Cattlemens Picnic

Marie Gibson riding bronc 1927 at a "Cattleman's Picnic" (Australian rodeo)
COURTESY OF ANN MARIE STAMEY

the fury of the damned. The rider, a woman, wears a bandage about her jaw. She is buffeted and tossed like dust in a storm. Suddenly she shoots from the saddle as though ripped by a mighty, invisible hand. As she plunges into the dirt, the bronco wheels about. There is fire in his eyes. "Marie!" a scream shrills through the arena, but it dies away in a sigh of relief. The woman had jerked her head in the nick of time. The hoofs missed and the bronco is boxed by the other horses.

Marie Gibson . . . is a rodeo veteran and one of the most color-ful cowgirls who ever slapped a quirt across a bronco's flank. . . . You'd swear she was Tom Mix, Buffalo Bill, Davey Crockett and Billy the Kid in female garb.

Her sons, Lucien and Andre, confirmed the description later when looking over bucking stock with other contestants. After discussing their own ability when they would spot a really rank bronc, the boys would say, "Well, if we can't ride him, our mother can!"

One of Marie's specialties early in her career was to ride any horse no one had been able to stay on during the rodeo. She would pass a hat around, and the crowds began to pay more attention as she rode the worst outlaw broncs.

The rules for women riders were the same as for men, and each cowgirl drew from the same bucking stock as the cowboys. In the original informal ranch rodeos, riders rode until they were bucked off or the animal quit bucking, whichever came first. In the organized rodeos, the time to the whistle was ten seconds for men and eight seconds for women. (Today's times are eight for men and six for women.)

Once mounted, the horse was controlled with one rein, which had to be held six inches above the horse's neck with either hand, the other held high in the air. The rider was disqualified if she or he grasped the horse's mane or "pulled leather," changed hands on the reins, wrapped the reins around a hand, or lost a stirrup. Some rodeos allowed women to use two reins and to ride hobbled.

The road was long and the life was not all glamour. Alice Greenough wrote, "We slept in tents most of the time. There were no motels. So we had our own bedrolls and our own washpan or water bucket and coffeepot. . . . We lived off our winnings. Lots of times it was just day money—twenty or thirty dollars if you won first place. . . ."

Cowboys and cowgirls not only had travel expenses in following the circuit, but they also had to pay their own entry fees, usually ten dollars but sometimes up to twenty-five dollars, a substantial sum in those days. Many rodeos, such as Madison Square Garden, required a fee for each event entered.

Some rodeo promoters took advantage of the traveling cowgirls and cowboys. Nicknamed "bloomers," these men traveled to smaller communities, advertising heavily for contestants, and they often charged higher entry fees. But then, just before the end of the rodeo, they would take the entry fees and gate receipts and skip town.

Marie Gibson wrote about such an incident in 1927, where she'd ridden in a show in Lexington, Kentucky. "I won 340 dollars and it did not pay up. It sure hit me hard . . . I may have to go to work here for a few weeks. . . ." Marie was trying to support her husband and children back home in Havre, after their crops had failed and they were unable to get a loan for spring planting.

At another rodeo in Los Angeles, Marie rode seven horses in one day and seventeen over the nine-day event. Her prize checks bounced, not an uncommon incident in the rodeo world. Another time, a Nelson, British Columbia, promoter left town owing her $325—a big sum for her in those days. She chased him halfway across Alberta but wasn't able to catch up with him.

On a more positive note, Marie was one of the only persons to make money from the ill-fated Dempsey-Gibbons boxing match in Shelby, Montana, on July 4, 1923. She rode in a rodeo held in conjunction with the fight and won a prize. Unfortunately, when she went to the bank to cash her check, the bank had run out of money. Marie received her pay anyway, from the bank's gold reserve.

Rodeo riders were a close-knit group and helped each other when they could. "If one fellow had ten dollars, you had five of it," Alice Greenough said, "[or] if you were out of money and needed a tire for your car . . . some old boy [who] had fifteen or twenty dollars, he'd come and say . . . 'You'd better use this to get yourself a tire.'"

Marie Gibson typified the type of life for the early twentieth-century cowgirl. From her first rodeo in Havre in 1917, she plunged into the North American rodeo circuit and began the long, hard, bruising climb to the title of World Champion Cowgirl Bronc Rider. After Havre, Marie participated in Canadian rodeos in British Columbia, Medicine Hat, Calgary, Moose Jaw, Regina, and all stops in between. Later she would travel all over the United States, competing in every major show in the country.

Women in rodeo and Wild West shows were a novelty. People in the cities were enamored with Westerners and came out in throngs, especially to watch the women ride.

After her recognition by royalty at the 1919 Saskatoon rodeo, Marie Gibson's next major highlight was being invited to participate in Tex Austin's nine-day New York City rodeo at Madison Square Garden in 1923. The following spring Austin made arrangements to take his performers to London for the thirty-day British Empire Exhibition at Wembley Stadium.

Marie joined 165 men and women performers, including Vera McGinnis, Bonnie McCarroll, Tad Barnes, and Florence Fenton.

London news writers, many of whom had just learned what a rodeo was, described the shows in exaggerated detail, informing the public about the feats and antics of the "queer and romantic men and women from the west." An advance story declared "'Hell-on-Hind-Legs' will soon be accepted in London as meaning rodeo. It's the cowboys' name for it."

Another wrote: "When the big bunch of cowpunchers arrives from America it will not be only at Wembley that their weird and picturesque personalities will make themselves felt. They are expected to make shopping raids on Bond Street and other West End centers. With their broad brimmed hats, chaps and spurs, they should create not a little interest."

Intense excitement created unheard of sales for "Wild West" periodicals and novels, and enormous crowds attended the opening performance.

Tex Austin, the consummate showman, had his performers decked out in their Western gear as they walked or rode down the gangplank.

Marie wrote in letters home during this trip: "Every afternoon and night there was the Grand Entry in which they introduced the judges . . . and Mr. Tex Austin, the world's greatest promoter, then the cowboys and cowgirls who had come to Wembley at their own expense. . . ."

She described the events:

[First on the program was] bareback bronc riding . . . 11 entries. [This] is when a cow boy comes out of the chute with a loose rope or a surcingle around the horse's belly. Next was fancy roping by the trick ropers, such as roping 4-5 horses at one time (while the roper was) standing on [his or her] head, or spinning two and three ropes at one time, one with their teeth and one in each hand.

Next was the cowgirl bronc riding [by six or seven contes-tants] who are the [most] fearless . . . riding wild horses just like the men do.

No. 4 was the breakaway steer roping contest . . . 9 steer ropers each performance. Breakaway steer roping is when a cowboy ropes a wild steer or horse and the end of his or her rope is tied with a small string. When the animal hits the end it breaks.

Last came the girls' trick and fancy riding [with nine trick riders].

Marie described some of the tricks: "standing up on the saddle, going under [the horse's] belly at full speed, going under his neck, laying across his neck with hands and feet free. . . . The Russian drag, hanging with one foot, your head and hair dragging while at full speed . . ."

Marie performed her trick and bronc riding skills every day despite several injuries, which should have put her in the hospital. One stunt she performed consisted of standing upright in the saddle while the horse ran at full gallop. Then she swung under its belly, around the horse's neck, and back up into the saddle. The first week the horse fell and rolled on her, and she dislocated her knee. She had it wrapped, and a friend helped her on her horse for the grand entry the next day. "I could sit in my saddle and ride without it hurting me too much, so I decided I could ride my bucking horse when the lady bronc event was called."

The men told her she was being foolish, but "when my name was called I was Johnny-on-the-spot."

Marie was able to climb up on the chute and drop down on the horse with help from "the boys." The bronc came sailing out of the chute, one of the worst horses she'd ever ridden, and all she could hear was "Ride 'im, Marie!" in the cheers from her fellow riders. When the whistle blew, she was helped off the horse by the pickup men and escorted out of the arena, where she could watch the rest of the rides. Even though her knee hurt terribly, she was glad she had done it, because she ended up winning "day money" with that ride.

"I really didn't want to ride anymore," she confessed later, "but there I was, all alone in a foreign country and no money to get home until I earned it."

So Marie came back later for more trick riding. "That was the toughest for me. Every once in awhile my knee would slip out of joint," and when she stepped off her horse afterward, she felt it go again.

"I went to a doctor to have it reset. He told me to lay off, but I had two days to rest, so I rode again. I had to have help saddling and mounting and they had to carry me from the stadium, but any prize money I might be able to get looked powerfully good to me," she wrote. "And for just a shilling a day I got transported to and from the arena in a wheelchair. Felt like a celebrity. That beat walking any day."

Because of that dislocation, she suffered further falls and injuries. The pain became so bad that sleeping was nearly impossible. Marie said, "I laid awake at night feverish in my hotel and for hours stared at the reflection of the street lamps that shone on the wall. And I wondered if I would be all right by the next afternoon's performance."

Without the help of her landlady, she was unable to dress herself. When the pain became too severe, she soaked in the bathtub, and one morning she awakened still in the tub.

Other cowgirls were injured too, Marie wrote, but after being treated they would get right back on and ride again. A newspaper article told of an injury to Anita Studnick, "a cowgirl who specialized in encounters with bucking horses, was carried the length of the arena by her vicious mount and thrown over his head. The injury was a broken collar bone."

Another rider, who had a horse fall on her and wrenched her neck in a relay race, received a letter from a woman who wrote she was sorry it had not broken her neck and killed her. The woman lambasted the cowgirl and all her "barbarian friends" who were so cruel to the animals.

In the course of events, a couple of steers broke legs and had to be shot. The Animal Protective League put out a pamphlet denouncing rodeo as "too dangerous." Tex Austin and the riders responsible for the injuries were arrested.

Marie Gibson leading horse given to her by the Prince of Wales, at Wembley in England COURTESY OF ANN MARIE STAMEY

There was a trial, the courtroom was packed, and it was front-page news every day. The case was dismissed, with the judge ruling that rodeo was not a form of cruelty to animals but all a part of working Western life, and if an animal was injured, it was quickly and humanely put out of pain.

"Of course, fox hunting did not look cruel to the Lords," Marie commented.

One of the London newspapers wrote, "When asked if rodeos were cruel, American trick rider Tad Lucas answered, 'Yes! But only for the cowboys and cowgirls.'"

But most of the English people were supportive of the performers and sent Marie letters, some addressed "To the Lame Cowgirl," congratulating her on her rides and her spunk. Others swarmed around her asking for autographs, and some offered to pay her bus or train fare while the troupe traveled.

Marie received a letter from a Dr. Gibson of Aldershot, who said he had relatives in America and wondered if Marie might be a relative of his brother John in Alberta. "I was," she wrote. "I had married his son."

Dr. Gibson came to meet her and they "had a wonderful time" getting acquainted. He told Marie he didn't want anyone with the name Gibson to be alone and without care for her injuries.

The performers were nearly mobbed when they went out onto the streets of London. Eager crowds followed them, asking for autographs. One boy, about age ten, walked twenty-five miles to see the performance. He approached one of the men. "Please, Cowboy, I would love to see the rodeo and I got no money." The rider got a burlap sack, put the boy in it, and carried him inside the arena over his shoulder.

During their stay in London, the cowgirls and cowboys were invited to several parties put on by English royalty—lords and ladies, princes and princesses. "They showed us the time of our life," Marie wrote.

One party's theme was "Bucking Horse Palace." Marie again met the Prince of Wales and danced with him. "We spent a lot of time talking," Marie wrote, and she was able to meet the queen, who asked her to tell about the prince riding after the rodeo ceremonies in Saskatchewan in 1919. "It was a lovely afternoon," Marie added.

Parties, dances, and sightseeing kept them all busy and in awe when they weren't riding. "Everything imaginable was to be seen," she said. Marie also went to Paris to visit friends. "There was something new to see every day. Never too old to learn."

Marie is said to have spoken five languages: French, Belgian, Cree, and Russian, as well as English, and was described as having a French accent.

The riders took several of the royals on a tour of the arena and chutes, showed them the horses and steers, and answered their many questions.

The troupe was pleased with the "wonderful crowd of people attending the shows," the smallest of which was around thirty-five thousand and largest up to one hundred thousand. Wembley Stadium was "the best stadium I've ever worked," Marie wrote.

After three weeks the show closed at Wembley, and Bea and Tommy Kirnan organized a show at the London Coliseum, then on to Dublin, Paris, and Brussels.

The troupe set sail for home around the seventh of July, and according to a news story of the departure, "there were boisterous scenes when the large party of cowboys and cowgirls embarked at the Royal Albert dock. The cowboys took with them many souvenirs, including several pigs, 12 dogs, two turtles and a rooster." Marie had also been given the gift of a horse by the Prince of Wales. She wrote she was happy to head "for the good old U.S.A. I was sure glad to come home once more."

As soon as Marie returned to the States, she and several others from the troupe set off for Cheyenne Frontier Days in Wyoming. She arrived one day late, and instead of riding one horse, she rode two. Crippled as she was from her London adventure, she nevertheless rode to the finish in a sensational battle on her broncs and won the Women's World Bronc Riding Championship award.

In quick succession the usual round of summer rodeos and stampedes followed. In Omaha a cowgirl was injured in the chute as she mounted the notorious horse Blue Dog, who reared and crushed her against the fence. Many men and women had attempted to ride Blue Dog and failed. Marie volunteered to ride the outlaw bronc. She mounted and rode him across the arena, proving once again that she could conquer the worst. Keyed up over the accident, the crowd went wild over Marie's ride.

In Great Falls in the summer of 1925, Marie was injured again. She had ridden a tall, rangy horse that gave her no challenge. She demanded to ride a "real horse" and made a bid for Scar Face after he'd hurled a rider to the dust.

Catching her foot in the fence as the horse came out of the chute, Marie's boot was torn half off. Off-balance now, she was thrown to the ground. The horse then whirled half around and lashed out at Marie lying on the ground, hitting her just above the eye and on her arm. A fraction of an inch closer, and her career would've ended.

Marie would not give up, however, and the next day rode another bronc, using only one foot in the stirrup because of the injury to the other. The crowd hailed her as heroine of the day for her nerve and skill.

Then, at a rodeo in San Antonio in 1928, she rode a sorrel, Wild Fire, who after three jumps, turned a somersault on top of her. Marie was carried unconscious from the arena. The doctor at the first-aid station administered ammonia and whiskey and was going to send her to the hospital. She refused and continued with the rodeo, despite a head so swollen her hat didn't fit. Then she rode in the relay race but remembered little about the race, only the ringing in her ears, occasional surges of pain, and swaying in the saddle. Later she did go to the hospital and discovered she had a broken jaw, which had to be wired shut.

She would meet Wild Fire again, and the next time rode him to top money, even though she injured her knee coming out of the chute.

Marie Gibson striking a pose, 1927 World Champion Bronc Rider, Madison Square Garden COURTESY OF ANN MARIE STAMEY

"Well, it's all in the game," Marie wrote in her journal. "If you want to keep at it you got to take it as it comes. It's a good life, lots of sport if you don't weaken."

Marie went on to win the Women's World Bronc Riding Championship at the Cheyenne Frontier Days in 1925 and the world championship title at Madison Square Garden in 1927 and 1931.

CHAPTER FOUR

The Ride Continues

*"A woman is like a tea bag—you can't tell how
strong she is until you put her in hot water."*
—ELEANOR ROOSEVELT

After Fannie Sperry's first successful bronc ride at age fourteen, she was hooked. She and her best friend, Christine Synness, egged each other on and convinced their parents to let them ride at another exhibition in Wolf Creek. Each girl took her own wild horse she had captured herself, but Fannie was horrified to see Christine's brothers "hobble" or tie her stirrups together under the horse's belly. This was a common practice to make it easier for women to stay in the saddle—once she put her feet in the stirrups, it was like being tied onto the horse. But that also meant she couldn't get off the horse without help.

Having learned to ride like a man, Fannie preferred riding "slick," stirrups not hobbled, one rein and one hand free. "It [hobbling] is too dangerous! She [Christine] could get hung up," she protested. Fannie later wrote, "Mine is the reputation of being the only woman rodeo rider who rode her entire career unhobbled. I confess it is a record I am proud of."

Besides, she explained, "I never have been able to consider it sporting to ride hobbled, for it isn't giving the horse a fifty-fifty chance."

That day, Fannie rode "slick," competing evenly with the men, and when the exhibition was over, she was declared the winner. The organizer, Dave Anson, passed his hat and gave Fannie $2.35 in "winnings."

Although her mother declared that Fannie was not to put on such a "risky and public display" again, there was no stopping the young cowgirl. When Anson approached her the next year for the Fourth of July rodeo, she did respect her mother's wishes and turned him down for bronc riding, but she suggested he put on a pony-express race, like the ones Buffalo Bill Cody ran.

He agreed. This show differed from Cody's in that the racers rode thoroughbreds and the women had to change horses four times during the race, at times even changing their own saddles. Christine won that first race, and Anson invited them to sign up for the bucking events at the state fair.

"Why not?" Christine replied.

Fannie's mother gave her daughter a sharp look.

"Please, Ma," Fannie pleaded. "I can't quit riding. Besides, I'm the best. Everyone says so. I can't quit now." Her mother reluctantly agreed.

In October 1903 the Montana State Fair in Helena added two fifteen-year-old girls to the roster of bucking-horse riders. Both did well and began receiving invitations to ride in other fairs, roundups, and stampedes, sponsored by the Capital Stock and Food Company of Helena.

Some of the seasoned riders grumbled about women riding in men's events, saying things like, "It don't make us look too good when you sage hens ride our broncs," but Fannie and Christine ignored the comments and continued to ride.

Walter Wilmot, a show promoter from Butte, offered Fannie a contract for one hundred dollars a week plus expenses. At her urging, he also signed Christine Syness and Dorothy and Margaret Getts of Cascade. For the next several years, the "Montana Girls" enjoyed traveling the country as champion relay racers.

One newspaper article from Grand Rapids, Michigan, described the five foot, seven inch, 125-pound Fannie:

The daring girl is a typical daughter of the Montana Ranches. She is of medium height, lithe, supple and graceful. Her pretty face is bronzed by the sun and winds of the west. . . . She rides ordinarily with the easy, graceful swing of the range rider, but when in a race she sits far up on her mount's withers, . . . with her head along the horse's neck, and skirts held as closely as possible to the racer's sides, that as little resistance as possible may be offered by the wind.

The possibility of spills—especially when the riders dismounted at high speed or leapt from one horse to another at full gallop—created spectator excitement at the races. Although Fannie escaped injury, at one race in the Midwest, Christine's horse charged out of the chute with its blindfold still on and crashed through the fence. She escaped with only a few bruises, however.

Their experience was not all danger and injury, however. Fannie later related a story about one race where a man dressed in a wig and women's clothing took the place of a woman rider who'd had too much to drink. All the women beat him. "He just didn't have the knack for swinging on and off. We teased him and called him 'Miss Wigs.'"

Before Wilmot took the girls on tour, he convinced Fannie to appear in a Wild West show at Butte's Columbia Gardens amusement center. In addition to racing, he talked her into riding a bronc, an outlaw horse named Tracy.

The *Butte Miner* reported: "If there ever was an imp of his satanic majesty incarnated in the disguise of a horse, Tracy is one. Tracy bounded into the limelight, carrying Miss Sperry. Miss Sperry may be a broncho buster, and she proved she is game to the core . . . but she had about as much chance to ride Tracy as Jim Jeffries [a well-known Montana heavyweight boxer] would have of earning a decision in a bout with a circular saw."

When the bronc came out of the chute, he suddenly stopped cold in his tracks and launched Fannie over his head. The *Miner* continued: "She made several revolutions in the air, and then struck the ground with a dull thud. Women screamed, for it seemed that the frail equestrienne had been dashed to death. But Miss Sperry arose gamely, and approached the black demon, who . . . was savagely pawing up the dirt. . . . It was a rare exhibition of grit, and two thousand voices howled their approval."

Fannie tried to remount, but the men in the arena would not let her. Later a cowboy rode Tracy, after which the bronc broke away from the cowboys, crashed through the stockade, and sent a spectator hurling through the air and to the hospital with a broken leg.

During her travels with Wilmot and also the J. Ellison Carroll Wild West Show of Texas, Fannie began regularly exhibiting bucking broncs as well as relay riding.

The Montana Girls won many races, and Fannie set race records and won numerous awards, including a medal for riding in a twenty-four-mile relay at the Minnesota State Fair. Despite the rigors of tough competition and traveling, Fannie seemed to thrive. She was doing what she loved best—working with horses. But in 1907 their promoter decided to take another business opportunity elsewhere and get out of racing.

Then, at Helena's Lewis and Clark Anniversary Celebration in 1907, Fannie entered a bucking horse competition. Defeating other women in the contest, she won a gold medal and was declared Lady Bucking Horse Champion of Montana, spurring her on to compete nationally in bronc riding.

Fannie's next big thrill was going to the newly organized Pendleton Roundup in 1910. There she met bronc rider Bertha Kaepernick Blancett—the first woman to compete against men in Cheyenne, in 1887—and Lucille Mulhall, Fannie's idol since she'd read about her in *Wild West* magazine.

The sport of rodeo riding was still relatively new, and the number of women rough-stock riders was especially small, so Fannie's reputation spread.

In 1912 Guy Weadick, an American trick roper who participated in the Miller Brothers 101 Ranch Real Wild West Show, organized the first Calgary Stampede. He invited Fannie to compete in the rodeo, along with several other top women competitors, including his wife Florence (also known as Flores) LaDue, Lucille Mulhall, Bronc-Busting Champion Goldie St. Clair of Wyoming, Bertha Blancett of Arizona, Dollie Mullins, and Hazel Walker of California. He enticed Fannie by saying she could probably win "some big money" and "entries for the Ladies is free."

An estimated eighty thousand people attended the first Stampede parade, an astonishing number, considering Calgary's population at the time was just over sixty thousand people. The *Calgary Herald* reported that one hundred thousand attended the six-day event: the first large-purse (twenty thousand dollars) rodeo and a milestone in rodeo history.

As Fannie and her mother arrived, they were horrified to learn that a wild bronc, Red Wing, had just thrown and stomped a cowboy to death. Leaden skies and relentless rain reflected the mood of the gathering. On Fannie's first day her bronc seemed immediately defeated by the muddy quagmire; he merely crowhopped a bit and then came to a standstill.

The next day Fannie drew a wild bronc who gave her the opportunity to show off her skills, but Goldie St. Clair had made a spectacular ride that day and was favored to win. Fannie needed an edge.

Then, on the last day of the rodeo, Fannie drew a slip of paper with the name of her bronc: Red Wing. Chills surely must have raced up her spine as she read that.

Despite the bronc's recent history, Fannie felt her draw was lucky—such a notorious horse could add points to her score. The crowd gasped as her ride was announced.

Fannie positioned herself in the saddle, all the while talking to the horse and trying to stroke his mane. "Okay, Red Wing, let's make a name for both of us," she said. "Let 'er buck!"

Red Wing came out of the chute on his hind legs, bucking, side-stepping, and twisting. Fannie's signature black braids bounced to the rhythm of the horse.

Fannie's ride stunned the crowd, and they whistled and clapped and stomped their boots on the wood bleachers. She had surpassed

Goldie's earlier ride, and this would go down in rodeo history as one of the best rides ever made by a man or a woman. She was crowned Lady Bucking Horse Champion of the World, winning one thousand dollars in cash, a three-hundred-dollar gold belt buckle, and a hand-tooled saddle.

Fannie swept off her hat and bowed. Then she searched the stands for her mother, Rachel, and spotted her sitting in the royal box with the Duke of Connaught (the governor-general of Canada).

Later a reporter asked Fannie if she was scared when she came out of the chute atop that killer bronc. She replied, "You just forget about being scared when you ride horses."

When asked by the Stampede officials what she planned to spend her winnings on, she told them, "I'm going to buy a piece of railroad land for my father." Her new friends at the Stampede passed the hat and presented her with another eight hundred dollars to put toward the land.

Following her success at Calgary, Fannie became an even bigger celebrity in Montana and was much in demand at fairs and horse shows. Her fame and striking looks attracted many would-be suitors, but as "Kid" Young, a Blackfoot Valley rancher remembered, "Beaus stood in line like kids at a Saturday matinee to get a chance to dance with Fannie. You were lucky if you ever got a turn. But none of the young fellows turned Fannie's head. She was too interested in broncs and arena excitement to care about dates."

But at the Deer Lodge Fair in 1912, she met Bill Steele, a man ten years her senior, who worked as a rodeo clown and was as interested in rodeo as Fannie. He was also the first man who'd captured Fannie's interest. They were married April 16, 1913.

The *Helena Herald* reported the event:

Miss Fannie Sperry Wedded to Horseman
World's Champion Woman Bronco Buster Married to W. S. Steele
Miss Fannie E. Sperry of Beartooth was married here yesterday afternoon to Wallace S. Steele, a horseman of Deer Lodge. The

wedding took place in the apartments of relatives in the Diamond Block. Mr. and Mrs. Steele will reside on Mr. Steele's large ranch near Deer Lodge.

Although Fannie normally preferred to wear well-worn divided leather skirts, on her wedding day she wore a deep-blue gabardine gown with a high lace collar, a flounce that concealed a plunging neckline, and a red rose corsage Bill had presented her.

When Fannie was asked later in life if it was love at first sight, she laughed. "I don't remember! [But] thank God the man who did love me . . . was a horseman, or our marriage would have been doomed before we started."

Fannie and Bill spent their honeymoon at a roundup at the Elliott Ranch near Deer Lodge and then continued rodeoing with C. B. Irwin's Wild West Show.

At a rodeo in Sioux City, Iowa, Fannie drew the saddle bronc Hot Shot. As she rode him to a standstill, he stumbled, fell, and pinned her. The crowd gasped, but Fannie rose, stood uncertainly for a moment, then fainted in Bill's arms.

Despite a badly sprained hip and back from that event, Fannie won her second Woman's Champion Bronco Buster title at Winnepeg later that summer, winning one thousand dollars and elevating her status back home as Montana's most popular athlete. She also easily won Montana State Lady Bucking Horse Champion again in Miles City in 1914 and came in second to Bertha Blancett at the Pendleton Roundup.

Fannie said later, "I never turned down a horse in my life, but I never disproved the saying, "Tain't a rider never been throwed, nor a horse that can't be rode.'"

The next year Bill and Fannie organized their own Wild West show and stock company. With her prize money from the Miles City Roundup in 1914, Fannie ordered a split riding skirt of brown-and-white calfskin from Al Furstnow, a well-known Miles City saddle maker. Wearing her fine new skirt and mounted on Silvertail in her

Fannie and Bill Steele show off her championship buckle COURTESY OF VIOLA HILGER NELSON

prize saddle, Fannie was ready to headline in the Powder River Wild West Show. (This riding skirt is still in excellent shape and on display at the family museum near Helena.)

44

Bill rode ahead around the state, promoting the shows, and because Fannie was a hero in Montana, people flocked from miles around to see her ride. Fannie showcased her skills on fast horses and bronc riding, and Bill offered twenty-five dollars to anyone in the audience who could ride the same bucking horses his wife did. Seldom did he have to pay.

Also putting on shooting exhibitions, Fannie would shoot the ashes off Bill's cigar and break china eggs he held between his fingers.

In 1915 the Steeles performed at the Rocky Mountain Stampede at Banff, Alberta, and the next year traveled with the Passing of the West show, which included rodeo stars Ben "PackSaddle" Greenough (Alice and Margie's father), Lucille Mulhall, and Vera McGinnis.

After this show ended, Guy Weadick invited the Steeles to New York City at the Sheepshead Bay Speedway Stampede. Fannie competed in bronc riding against seven of the best cowgirls in the country and ran relay races against the nation's top women racers. She also rode Brahma bulls and was one of the few riders who successfully rode the outlaw bronc Midnight.

Honored guest Theodore Roosevelt told the *New York Times* he was impressed with the female riders, but he was not keen on women riding bucking horses; he was afraid they would seriously injure themselves.

On the way home they performed in Chicago, Milwaukee, and Kansas City. In Chicago they met and performed with Lucille Mulhall, Buffalo Bill Cody, and Bill Pickett, the famous black cowboy who introduced "bulldogging" to rodeo. Then, at a Milwaukee fair, Fannie wowed the audience by riding six consecutive broncs.

In 1917 Fannie and Bill performed in the Great Northern Montana Stampede in Havre, where Fannie met with tough competition but won the bucking horse contest. Then they went on to Cheyenne's Frontier Days rodeo and the Calgary Stampede. It was the last year Fannie and Bill participated in large-scale rodeos. In 1919 they bought a ranch at Jackson Creek southeast of Helena and for the next few years just traveled Montana with their own small show.

Fannie continued to compete until she was thirty-eight, but after twenty years of being a rodeo performer, dreams of future championships had lost their appeal and the applause of the crowds wasn't enough anymore.

After meeting Dick Randall, who owned the OTO Guest Ranch near Gardiner, Bill came up with the idea to start a dude ranch. "He and his wife take in city folks and show them how to ride, hunt, and fish," Bill told Fannie. "Lots of ranchers are making money packing dudes into the backcountry. The way I see it, no reason we can't do the same."

Fannie jumped at the idea. "I think we could. We have all the qualifications."

In 1925 they sold their Jackson Creek property and bought a ranch on Arrastra Creek near Helmville, in Bill's favorite valley. Deer and elk tracks welcomed them to a hunters' retreat nestled among giant pine, fir, and tamarack in the mountain wilderness.

After the Bozeman Roundup in September, Fannie hung up her spurs, although she continued giving exhibitions into her fifties. A former neighbor in the Beartooths lamented, "The cowgirls' bucking won't amount to much without you."

"Not many women in bronc riding these days anyway. Most of the stampedes have quit the cowgirls' bucking-horse event," Fannie told him. "They say the sport is too dangerous for women."

The Steeles opened their guest ranch that fall, and Fannie became the first licensed female outfitter in Montana. To supplement their income while they built up their business, Bill got a job with the Montana Fish and Game Department to stock area streams and lakes with fish.

That left Fannie to guide their visitors into the Rocky Mountain wilderness, which she continued until well into her seventies. She loved teaching inexperienced riders to feel the partnership between them and their horses, to show them the contentment in this way of life and the beauty of the wild country.

The couple remained childless, except for Bill's son from an earlier marriage. Later, one of Fannie's nieces told *Montana* magazine writer Beth Judy she was "glad that Fannie married Bill, because she could keep on riding whenever she wanted. She wasn't going to go for raising kids and farming."

Inducted into the National Cowboy Hall of Fame in 1975 and the Montana Cowboy Hall of Fame in 1978, Fannie said, "Sometimes it takes a lot of grit to do what you want to do, but I can't see how people can stand the monotony of doing work at which they are not happy."

The 1920s continued to allow Montana's cowgirls to find fame and excitement in the arena, showing the world they could ride as well as the men.

A hardscrabble life, backbreaking work, and a sense of perseverance trained the Montana cowgirls for the danger and risk, as well as opportunity and excitement, of rodeo competition. Each one had her own difficulties to overcome to reach the pinnacle of her career.

CHAPTER FIVE

Cowgirl Life Is Not Easy

"Anything a cowboy can do, we can do and better."
—THE BRANDER SISTERS

The hot sun beat down on the teenage girl's back and sweat beaded on her forehead. She gripped the handles of the plow with blistered hands as it bit and bucked through the rocky earth on the steep hillside and then tipped over. Violet Brander tucked wisps of her reddish blond hair under her hat, wiped the perspiration from her face, set her legs wide, and tried to right the two-way plow. Although she stood an impressive five foot, eleven inches, she was of slender build. She groaned and struggled, but the plow wouldn't budge.

"Marg! Help!" she yelled to her younger sister, who pulled up behind her with another team of three horses and a disk. Between the two they finally got the plow back upright and continued preparing the twenty-acre field at Bradley, near Avon, Montana, for planting.

The Brander sisters, the fourth and fifth children of fifteen and the oldest daughters, were expected to pitch in with the housework, which included baking dozens of loaves of bread, washing clothes in a tub with a washboard, caring for the garden, and disciplining the younger children. When it came time to plant grain and harvest, cut, and stack hay, they did that too, as their three older brothers were helping their father as a sawyer in the woods.

To prove up the homestead, Vi later related, "Twenty acres [of steep and rocky hillsides] had to be plowed and seeded to crop." She and Marg did most of that work. "It was as hard to get it cut and stacked on top of the mountain as it was to get the land ready. During the winter we tramped up those steep hills in snow up to our waists to feed the stock we kept up there. It was bitterly cold and blizzardy, particularly in December, January, February and March, but we had to feed—if we hadn't, the stock would have starved! It's a good thing we were young and strong then."

Overcoming a life of poverty and backbreaking labor, these two "workhorses" developed a tough and fearless outlook. In addition to helping their mother with the farm, they worked at any job that would help keep the home place going and earn a few extra coins to support the family. "Life wasn't easy," they admitted.

In 1922, after a spat with their father, Vi, eighteen, and Marg, seventeen, rode bareback seventy miles cross-country to Bill and Fannie Steele's ranch at Montana City. Fannie greeted the two fresh faces with enthusiasm and invited them to stay for the summer. The girls worked for the Steeles, mowing, raking, and stacking hay for "keep and found" (board and room). Fannie, whom they had met and admired previously at a rodeo, also taught them to ride broncs.

"I never saw nobody who can talk to horses like you can, Fannie," Marg told the rodeo cowgirl. "How'd you get 'em to understand you like that?"

"I listen to them, I guess," Fannie explained. "I seem to know what they're thinking just from being around them all my life. I feel it in my bones, in my heart. I wouldn't know how to tell anybody. You have to get to know them. Takes time. And patience."

Marg and Vi listened well and would take Fannie's advice and teaching to heart to use in their future rodeo career.

After that summer, the sisters went to high school in Deer Lodge, where they worked as babysitters and housemaids for their board.

During the summers they worked shoulder to shoulder with men, earning one dollar for a ten-hour day doing farm and ranch work. One summer Vi and Marg also went to pick fruit in Washington for the unheard-of high pay of three dollars a day, and then they worked in a box factory in Oregon before returning to Montana to work with their brothers in the timber industry.

The sisters had found that the best way to make a living was to do men's work at men's pay. From dawn until dusk they ran a crosscut saw, felling the big trees, limbing, peeling, and skidding them to an area where they helped load them on vehicles to be hauled to a railroad siding at Bradley.

Helen Kay Brander Larson, another sister, wrote in the book *Let 'er Buck*:

> *Falling timber means bending over until your back feels as though it will never straighten again in weather so cold and miserable "tis not fit for man or beast to be abroad." Arms ache from the constant see-saw of the crosscut as it bites through the bark and wood until finally the shout of 'timber' rings out and the giant tree crashes to earth in a shower of pungent sawdust and splinters.*
>
> *Limbing is swinging a heavy two-bladed axe until your hands are cramped so tightly around the handle you have to pry each finger loose to let go. Peeling is the same thing except that an adze is used instead of an axe.*

But it was a job and meant money to eat and to buy clothes. Margaret and Violet were hard, conscientious workers, and their services were always in demand by ranchers in the nearby communities.

One summer after Vi and Marg graduated high school, they went to the Deer Lodge Rodeo, where the promoters asked them to ride an exhibition bronc as an added attraction. They said, "Sure," and it turned out to be the hit of the show. Learning that an eight-second ride could pay fifteen dollars, they began riding exhibitions at local rodeos.

Also at the Deer Lodge Fair, Vi discovered another talent. During the half-time show, a Texan gave a Roman Riding exhibition (standing with one foot each on the back of two horses). The man challenged the young cowgirl to a race. Vi had never done it before, but she was always eager to become the first woman to try something new. Tying a piece of twine between the two bridles of her horses, Vi jumped onto their backs, found her center of balance, and the race was on.

And she won.

"The crowd went crazy, like a touchdown at a football game," her niece, Linda Brander, said. "The headline could've been 'Local Girl Beats Pants Off Cocky Texan.'"

Her son, Marlin Gilman, said of his mother, "[She] had a terrific sense of balance. She could balance on horses while twirling two ropes at a time." Vi became adept at Roman racing and won over many men in this event during the years.

At another rodeo in Polson, the sisters met Paddy Ryan, a slight, five-foot bronc rider. He asked Vi to ride double on a steer with him. "I'll kick him under the chin from my seat on the neck if he gets to buckin' too hard. That way you won't have any trouble riding on his back."

Always game, Vi agreed. They made a successful ride, Vi had fun, and she thought it was easy. "If Paddy and I can do it, you and I can," she told Marg. And from that event, the Brander sisters' career was born. They claimed to be the only cowgirls in the world to ride the big Brahma steers double, Vi on the back and Marg on the neck.

"However," the five-foot, ten-inch Marg remembered, "I couldn't kick the steer under the chin—I was too tall. It was hard enough just keeping my long legs in place and him from jumping into my boots with me. Paddy was short—it was easy for him."

Vi and Marg rode in rodeos all over Montana, Colorado, and Utah, in Canada, and at the second annual World's Rodeo in Chicago. "It [rodeo] gave us the freedom to travel and work. Nobody got paid for 'women's work,'" Marg said.

That they risked their lives on each of these bucking animals apparently never entered the sisters' minds. But later in life Marg reminisced about one particular hair-raising ride when she had been told to take a "short hold" on the rope rein, which turned out to be bad advice. At the first lunge out of the chute, the bronc yanked the rein from her hand, leaving her with only the tip of it as a balance for the rest of the ride. The heavy horse lunged with its head and kicked back, while twisting its hindquarters. Since Marg was riding hobbled, she couldn't jump free. And with no rein to balance her, she was whipped back and forth on the fighting animal for what seemed an eternity. With one lunge she would hit the saddle horn and on the next, the cantle—over and over. Finally a pickup man was able to get close enough to take her off the bronc. By that time both her eyes were black and her body covered with bruises and abrasions. Marg admitted she had been lucky to escape alive.

"We always had to draw our horses right with the men," Vi said. "Sometimes we'd get a light, showy bronc, and the next time, one that was so rough he'd tear you to pieces, but look as though he wasn't bucking at all."

The sisters were seldom bucked off, however. Vi said the only time she was ever thrown from a bucking horse was when the cinch broke. "I thought I had it made, when saddle, me and all, went over the bronc's head and landed with a sickening crash on the ground."

A black Angus steer also piled the duo one time in Polson. "Most of the time it was harder getting off than it was getting on, particularly on the Brahmas," Vi said. "They have a six-foot horn spread and are vicious. They're prodded with an electric prod and a flank strap is drawn up tight around their middle . . . to make sure they'll buck. They're mad at the world even before you get down on 'em."

Vi wrote in an article for *Western Story* magazine, "Now about the wild steers, I'll tell you—they don't look so awfully hard to ride, but if you care to ride the next thing to a cyclone, just pick out a nice, long-horned Texas steer. . . . If he doesn't give you more thrills per second than you've ever had in your life, then I give up."

Steer riders rode with a loose rope or a leather surcingle—a long strap around the animal's middle—held with one hand (women were allowed to use two if they wanted). Often a cowbell was attached to the rope to help promote bucking. "If you can ride him over the deadline, which is only fifty feet, we riders take our hats off to you," Vi said. "If he does throw you, look for a high spot, *muy pronto,* for he's sure coming right back after you a-snorting and a-bellering."

The sisters also roped, bulldogged, did trick roping, and won a Wild Cow Milking contest over a field of male entries. As their rodeo career progressed, the Branders added relay racing to their repertoire. They collected horses no one wanted: Mickey, a thoroughbred high-strung mare the male owner couldn't handle; another mare, Polly, who was too rebellious for her former owner; and Buckles, a mustang with no known bloodlines who made up for lack of speed with spunk and stamina. Vi and Marg won many purses on their racing string.

The sisters garnered big headlines when they appeared in their home state. The *Montana Standard* in Butte reported:

> *With the distinction of having more girl bronc riders than any state, Montana has the only two girls who are expert in the dangerous pastime of bulldogging wild steers. The Brander Sisters of Avon, winners of various rodeo prizes, yesterday entered the list of contestants who will display skills in the big Butte Wild West show here. . . . Both Violet and Margaret Brander have entered the bulldogging contests as well as other dangerous stunts. . . . Other Montana girls who have filed as bronc riders, relay racers and fancy riders are Miss "Pete" Shipman of Cardwell, Ruth Martin of Bozeman, Alice Sisty of Camas, Edna Edwards of Red Lodge and Minnie Smith of Miles City.*
>
> *The Butte Rodeo Association was admitted to membership in the Rodeo Association of America . . . and the association is one of the four listed as Class A. Other Class A shows are Madison Square Gardens, New York; Cheyenne, Wyo., and Pendleton, Ore.*

Bulldogging is also known as steer wrestling, in which the rider chases a steer, drops from the horse to the steer, then wrestles it to the ground by twisting its horns. It takes a lot of strength to wrestle a 750- to 1,000-pound steer. Only a few women ever competed in that event, and women's bulldogging contests never materialized nationally. Tillie Baldwin, originally from Norway, was the first in 1913, and Fox Hastings of Texas set a record time at the Fort Worth Rodeo in 1924.

"Anything a cowboy can do, we can do and better," became the Brander sisters' motto. If they had to give up on one thing, they tried something else.

"The old proverb of life is, 'Life is a gamble.'" Vi wrote in an article in *Western Story* magazine. "My proverb for rodeos is: 'A gamble with life.' From the moment a rider lowers himself off the chute onto the back of an outlaw horse or wild steer he never knows but what his minutes are limited. Some folks say, 'Oh, that's easy! They've only got to ride them (less than) one minute.' But let me tell you, that's one of the longest minutes you'll ever live. . . . It's one of the greatest sports on earth and one of the most hazardous. . . . But I wouldn't trade one second of my arena life for all the rest of my life put together."

"That girl'll never make sixteen."
—Hiram Brooks

Born December 1, 1913, in Terry, Montana, Bobby Brooks, like Fannie Sperry Steele, started riding at age three and broke her first horse at eight. Bobby spent her early life on the open range, when ranch country was just beginning to be fenced. Her father, Hiram, had settled in Montana after a trail drive from Texas. He was later elected sheriff of Prairie County, so Bobby and her two brothers were their mother's "ranch hands" on the family spread. Bobby's mother, Violet Butterfield (Brooks), was crowned the first Miss Montana, but she was also an avid rider and had ridden as a jockey for her father. Bobby followed in the footsteps of her mother with her love of horses and riding.

Named Lemeral Lenora at birth, Bobby was called "Lemmy" until her grandmother cut her hair and started calling her "Bobby." Hating her given name, she changed it legally when she turned eighteen.

Bobby broke her first horse at age eight, and when Bobby's dad watched his daughter ride broncs with such fearless determination, he muttered, "That girl'll never make sixteen."

Bobby recounted in an interview with the *Billings Gazette* later in life, "When I made it to sixteen, he said, 'I'll just bet anything she'll never make it to twenty-one.'"

But she did make it well past twenty-one, even though she admitted she was a bit reckless "or I wouldn't have been riding the horses I did." Bobby was ninety-one when she passed away, well known in Montana for her horse-training abilities.

Her adopted son, Gary Crowder, described her as "tougher than hell, but they didn't come any better than her at running horses. Bobby could ride a wolf."

When the indomitable young woman was about fifteen, she moved a herd of two hundred horses from Terry to Broadus (about one hundred miles) by herself, spending the night on her saddle horse's back, because "there were lots of rattlesnakes. I could hear them buzz," she related.

At sixteen Bobby married, but she said, "It didn't last. We weren't cut out to be man and wife. He was too much like my brothers."

The Brooks family moved to a ranch southwest of Jordan in 1929, at the beginning of several years of tough drought. It took endless work to keep their stock fed. In 1931, as a break from that hardscrabble routine, Bobby and her brothers went to the Wolf Point Stampede.

Her brothers won one hundred dollars riding broncs, but Bobby went off to have some fun of her own. "I took twenty-five dollars and went to gambling. And I lost it all." Disappointed and embarrassed, she dreaded going home to face her mother's wrath.

"I was moping around when the stock promoter came up to me. 'I understand you are quite a hand with rough horses,' he said, and offered me twenty-five dollars if I could ride a bronc to the whistle." Bobby accepted the offer and earned back her lost money.

In 1937, at the age of twenty-four, Bobby became one of Montana's women bucking horse riders in rodeo and competed for about ten years.

"Girls ridin' rodeo was the wrong thing to be a doin', but I didn't care what 'they' thought—I did it anyway," Bobby related in *I'll Ride That Horse*. "Mother encouraged me to do whatever I wanted."

She said they didn't travel like the Greenoughs but mostly rode Montana rodeos.

When Bobby was in her late teens, she was "pretty rowdy and competed with her brothers," according to Gary Crowder. They teased her about her male-dominated sport of bronc riding. "Being a lady is a different thing," they said. "It's not your world. You couldn't do that."

Never one to be told what she could or couldn't do, Bobby replied, "Oh yeah?" She proceeded to sell a couple of horses, moved to Billings, and enrolled in beauty school. While there she "tuned up a horse" for a friend, never losing touch with her roots.

She graduated from beauty school, but, she later stated, "That was the closest to being a beautician I ever got. Shortly after graduation she was walking down the street when she heard someone yell, "Hey, Bobby!" It was a man she'd met on the rodeo circuit, and he asked if she'd like to ride some green-broke horses for the Miles City Bucking Horse Sale.

Bobby needed some money, so she said, "Sure." She wrote a postcard home asking her folks to send her saddle, and she went to work riding throughout the sale. One horse bucked over backward and broke her saddle, but she kept going. Later the man who had hired her brought her a new Hamley saddle from Pendleton, Oregon.

She was hooked on competition and continued winning a house full of trophies and awards throughout her life.

CHAPTER SIX

The 1930s: Beginning of the End

"We live each day as if it's our last."
—FANNIE SPERRY STEELE

Dust devils rose from the corrals amid a blistering ninety-six degrees on September 19, the first day of the 1929 Pendleton Roundup. Marie Gibson wiped perspiration from her forehead as she watched from the chutes with Bertha Kaepernik-Blancett and several other cowgirls.

Bonnie McCarroll, from Boise, Idaho, was next up to ride in the women's saddle bronc exhibition. On her way to retirement with her husband, Frank, she had pleaded with him for "just one more ride."

The women watched Bonnie mount Black Cat with her stirrups hobbled, for reasons that are unknown and controversial to this day. Some say the Roundup officials required it; others say that since the cowgirls' saddle bronc contest was not a rodeo competition but an exhibition only, it wouldn't make sense for the Roundup committee to require this. Bonnie, like Montanans Marie and Fannie, usually rode "slick."

"That should not be allowed," Bertha remarked. "It is just 'suicide' to ride that way."

Frank accompanied Bonnie and lifted the diminutive cowgirl into the saddle, to the cheers of the crowd. She waved at her fans, planted her boots in the stirrups, secured her hat on her head, and nodded, ready for a spectacular last ride. The snubber pulled the gunnysack blindfold from Black Cat's eyes; the bronc lunged up and forward but lost his footing and fell.

Marie and the watching women gasped as the horse, trying to recover, went into a backward somersault with Bonnie trapped in the saddle, one foot still caught in the hobbled stirrups.

Following his instincts, the bronc leapt to his feet and continued to buck. Bonnie's head hung down, her body flopped limply, and her left foot was still caught in the stirrup. The pickup man desperately tried to grab hold of her. For six more horrible leaps and lunges, Bonnie's head hit the ground with sickening repetition until her boot finally came off and she lay unmoving on the ground.

Ollie Osborn, one of the cowgirls watching, later said, "I could hear that girl's head hit that ground, right there in the bleachers."

Bonnie McCarroll died eleven days later in a Pendleton hospital.

Marie Gibson was shaken to the core. She'd already lost a good friend, Louise Hardwick from South Dakota, three years earlier.

She commented to a newspaper writer, "You just never know, from [one] minute to the next, if you're going to answer that final roll call. You might say you take your life in your hands. We deplore the tragedy that takes human life, but we glory in the fine exhibitions. . . ."

Despite the danger, Marie continued to supplement the family's income with her riding skills into the 1930s, winning her second world championship title in women's bronc riding at Madison Square Garden.

Marie Gibson unfortunately proved the truth of Fannie Sperry Steele's words: "Rodeo teaches you that death is right around the corner and the 'now' is all you have, so make the most of it. It may be the old Anglo-Saxon creed, 'Eat, drink, and be merry for tomorrow you die' carried over into rodeo, but it fits. We live each day as if it's our last."

Nearing age forty, Marie was growing weary of the demanding rodeo life, many injuries, and time away from her family. She was considering "hanging up" her spurs to retire on her ranch and spend more time with her family.

Then Marie attended a rodeo in Idaho Falls on September 23, 1933, just before she planned to go to Madison Square Garden. She drew a wild, high-bucking bronc and gave a spectacular, successful ride. The whistle blew, signaling the pickup man to come pluck her off the back of the still-bucking horse. Just as he reached her, Marie's bronc turned, crashed into the pickup man's horse, and fell to the ground.

Her sons were with her that summer, and twenty-three-year-old Lucien was the first to reach her.

Marie's skull was fractured, and she died a few hours later.

One of Marie's own poems sums up her feelings about life:

> Let us ride together
> careless of the weather
> blowing mane and hair
> miles ahead, no cares
> sound of hoof and horses sniff
> trotting down the Milk River
> with the wind let's slip
> let us laugh together
> young one or old
> to the crack of the leather
> when it is cold
> break into a canter
> shout at chicken and rabbit
> running down the river trail
> steady hand and knee
> take the life of the country
> that's the life for me
> it would be a pity
> not to gallop free
> so we all ride together
> careless of the weather
> and let the world go by.

And words said at her funeral included: "She died as she lived, hearing the applause of the people."

A retired cowboy later told Marie Gibson's granddaughter, Ann Marie Stamey, "Life may have been tough for Marie, but she had a heck of a good time in rodeo anyway. It sort of gets in your blood."

What happened to Bonnie McCarroll in Pendleton in 1929 and then again to Marie Gibson in 1933 is credited with the beginning of the end for the rodeo and Wild West show cowgirls across the country.

But according to Steve Wursta in his documentary film *From Cheyenne to Pendleton,* the tide had begun to turn against cowgirls many years earlier. Wursta cites "difficulties with" Mabel Strickland of Washington, a ninety-eight-pound steer roper who set the world's record at Frontier Days in Cheyenne in 1924. Apparently she was too talented for her male competitors' taste. Cheyenne and Pendleton subsequently banned this cowgirl from competing against the men, and in 1926 Pendleton announced that it had eliminated competition for women in favor of paid exhibitions.

Pendleton's *East Oregonian* explained it this way: "Women now swim the English Channel and they can ride about as swiftly as can any man who ever walked, hence they do not require nor do they desire the same degree of attentiveness [as] when the Round-Up was young."

Wursta writes, "While on the surface this statement may not make much sense, it fits quite well with the pattern of social and economic changes that pitted the now conservative rural farming communities against the more liberal urban cities of the east after World War I.

"While it was the environment of the west that allowed young girls to escape the restrictive urban culture to develop the skills to be called 'cowgirls'. . . it was also the changing environment of the west that would remove women from the rodeo arena in favor of the cowboy."

Protective "knights-of-the-saddle syndrome," men's egos, and changing social mores, along with the following factors, contributed to the demise of women's rodeo by the 1940s:

- The formation of the all-male Rodeo Association of America (RAA)
- Financial difficulties resulting from the stock market crash and the Great Depression
- World War II

Following the 1929 incident, an article in the *Yakima Republic* represented the national sentiment: "Here is an instance of human injuries and death that impels the question of whether such a show is worth such a sacrifice."

The age-old question reared its ugly head once again: Should women be doing something so dangerous and physical as competing in rough-stock events? Only fifty years earlier, social attitudes had shifted to allow women to enter professions and engage in activities previously open only to men. Modernists argued that everyone would benefit by women's independence, while traditionalists insisted that marriage and domesticity were the core of women's identity—a debate that was revived by McCarroll's death.

Pendleton's rodeo board immediately ended women's bronc riding, even as an exhibition sport, and as one of the country's largest rodeos, that decision set a precedent other rodeos soon followed.

According to Milt Riske, author of *Those Magnificent Cowgirls*, at least one veteran promoter was of the opinion that the protective cowboys' arguments for women riders' rights actually worked against them and contributed to the demise of women's events.

The second factor that contributed to the decline of women's participation in rodeo was the Rodeo Association of America (RAA). Formed in 1929 to standardize events and regulations, its founding members made an effort to eliminate the "bloomers" and "fake rodeos" where the contests were staged and the promoters rotated the "victories" among themselves.

Part of this standardization included selecting which events would be included in all RAA-sanctioned rodeos, which had to include men's bronc riding, steer bulldogging, steer roping, and calf roping. This list did not include women's bronc riding. The organization did not specifically prohibit women riding, and left it up to local rodeo committees to include the event. But when the RAA later increased the list from four to eight sanctioned events, many rodeos included these new events at the expense of the women.

"When the RAA formed [the cowgirls] implored them to include women's events and make rules for them . . . for reasons we will never know, they refused," Mary Lou LeCompte, author of *Cowgirls of the Rodeo: Pioneer Professional Athletes*, wrote.

Ironically, it was the East that would temporarily save the rodeo cowgirl. Many Eastern rodeo promoters did not join RAA, and women's bronc riding and trick riding gained popularity in that part of the country. Montana's cowgirls benefitted, as witnessed by the world championships won by Marie Gibson and Alice Greenough in New York and Boston during the 1930s.

International rodeo flourished during the 1930s as well—in Europe, Australia, Cuba, and Mexico—and in 1932 a promoter invited Alice to go to Spain. "That year in Spain was one of the best I ever had," she related. Before each bullfight, she would ride the bull out of the chute and around the ring. Then the matadors took over their part of the show.

After Alice won her first championship in Boston in 1933, she was among several rodeo riders to perform in the White City Stadium in London. Family members recounted that Queen Mary joined Alice and the riders for tea at the stables. Because the tea was too strong for Alice, she asked for additional hot water. Her niece Christine Linn now has that gold lusterware pitcher that was later sent across the ocean aboard a ship with a friend of the queen's to present to "that little cowgirl" at Madison Square Garden.

Not long after Alice returned home from England, she was selected as the only woman in a group to go to Australia. She performed "all over the back country" during 1934 and 1935 at "cattlemen's picnics," as rodeos were called. She won the Cowgirls International buck-jumping contest (bronc riding) in Sydney in 1935 and 1939.

"If travel is educational, the cowgirls should have been awarded Masters' Degrees," Milt Riske wrote in *Those Magnificent Cowgirls*.

Alice was one of the professional cowgirls to enhance her income through endorsements, something few women athletes experienced during that era. The international successes enhanced the publicity at home. Most of the events paid huge prizes, with promoters paying all or part of the contestants' travel expenses, and helped add to the American cowgirls' earnings. While in Australia, Alice endorsed products from saddles to refrigerators, and later back home received several lucrative offers, including one for cigarettes. Although she was not a smoker, Alice signed the contract.

But the impact of Bonnie McCarroll's death and the RAA began to change the environment, leaving few options for women rodeo riders.

Even with the RAA's standardized rules, the problems of "crooks" in the business continued to flourish. Vi and Marg Brander learned this firsthand when they attended the World's Championship Rodeo in Chicago in 1932.

Marg later related, "Cowgirls from the North never had a chance. We drew our broncs the same as did the cowboys. The showy bucking horses that jumped high and bucked straight ahead always went to the southern girls. Northern cowgirls were allowed to win just enough to keep them riding for the nine days. [We] never got into the running for the championship money, even though the rodeo was billed as 'competitive.'"

Following this "fixed" rodeo, the sisters were nearly broke. Vi wanted to go on to Madison Square Garden, but Marg vetoed the idea, and they headed home to Montana in a Dodge roadster they had bought for $125 on the installment plan and just enough money for gas.

This practice of a promoter bringing his own troupe of performers who ended up being the "winners" persisted. Cowboys accused Col. William T. Johnson—who had developed the successful Madison

Square Garden and other Eastern rodeos—of distributing prize money mostly to himself. In 1936 they went on strike at the Boston Garden Rodeo and demanded a bigger share of the admissions proceeds for their prize money. Johnson finally gave in, and the cowboys formed the Cowboys Turtle Association (CTA), the forerunner of today's Professional Rodeo Cowboys Association (PRCA). The CTA was named, as the story goes, "because we were slow to organize but finally stuck our necks out."

Women joined the organization but were nonvoting members, and cowboys only rarely acted on the cowgirl's behalf, having declared in 1938 that women were "on their own." One exception was at the 1939 Fort Worth rodeo. Men did threaten to strike because the women's bronc riding competition had been dropped in favor of the "sponsor girls" event (more a beauty pageant than a competition). Leading the protest was a cowboy whose wife was a cowgirl bronc-riding representative to the CTA. The promoters finally agreed to allow a two-woman riding exhibition at one performance.

Unfortunately, two cowgirls putting on one exhibition ride did not encourage women's contests in future rodeos.

Women had joined the Turtles expecting to benefit from the riders' organization, and cowgirls like the Greenough sisters resented paying dues when they had no vote. But the CTA did improve conditions overall for the sport, eliminated dishonest promoters, and obtained more equal distribution of prize money, so the women perhaps felt that the improvements overshadowed the disadvantages.

Jane Burnett Smith earned her Turtle Association card.
COURTESY OF CAMILLE SMITH

66

"It would be easy to suggest that the women should have formed their own organization, but it is doubtful if many cowgirls would have been willing to defy their husbands to do so," wrote Mary Lou LeCompte in *Cowgirls of the Rodeo.* "The West, like the rodeo business, was a patriarchy, and most of the cowgirls had been raised under the stern control of their fathers. . . . The rodeo business had given these women a much freer and more exciting life-style, yet their fate still rested with powerful males: promoters, producers, judges, rodeo committees, husbands, and now the CTA-RAA."

Although several women tried to negotiate with their own local rodeo committees, they were in the minority in the sport. Even if all the cowgirls, along with all the cowboys married to women in the sport, had formed a group, they would not have been able to overcome the trend.

New promoters took over the Madison Square Garden and Boston Rodeos, and women were the biggest losers in this evolution of the sport. "The Singing Cowboy," Gene Autry, was one of the first promoters to develop a cadre of "sponsor girls." Once again "traditional" gender roles were asserted, and these sponsor contests focused on femininity rather than on athleticism.

Upper-class Easterners had a negative attitude toward female professional athletes and found amateur sports more socially acceptable, so the *Madison Square Garden* magazine took advantage of this and advertised these sponsor girls as strictly amateur, not competing for prize money. "These youthful beauties . . . are sponsored socially and otherwise by the localities they represent."

The sponsor girls idea was actually born in Stamford, Texas. In 1930 the town fathers wanted to help boost low moral that resulted from the Great Depression and try to preserve the history of the cowboy with the Stamford Cowboy Reunion. The first three-day reunion featured an all-male rodeo, but the following year the parade committee invited businesses from the surrounding area to sponsor a female contestant. These young women led the opening-day parade, and they demonstrated horsemanship by riding in a figure eight around barrels, the birth of barrel racing.

"It wasn't really a contest, because they were judged on their horse, their outfit . . . ," said rodeo historian LeCompte in an outtake from the documentary *From Cheyenne to Pendleton, the Rise and Fall of the Rodeo Cowgirl.*

Fellow historian Renee Laegreid adds, "The economy was down and do you want to bring women in to compete against men when they are feeling so badly already? So they said, no women, but we will have them there, as kind of, you know, eye candy. . . . So they are bringing beauty into it, for the first time."

In 1939 Everett Colburn, who now produced the Madison Square Garden event, invited the Texas Sponsor Girls to appear at his rodeo to garner publicity. The next year the women rode while Gene Autry sang "Home on the Range."

Autry formed his own rodeo company in 1941 and eventually took over Madison Square Garden, Boston Garden, and most of the other major rodeos throughout the country. The new formula, which combined patriotism and Western music with beautiful women riders, brought in more money than the traditional rodeos that included cowgirls' rough-stock events. For business reasons one of Autry's first actions was to discontinue the cowgirl bronc-riding contest, which had been a highlight of the Madison Square Garden Rodeo since its inception in 1922. Vivian White of Oklahoma was the last woman bucking horse champion at the Garden in 1941.

One of the "competitions" that resulted from that Stamford rodeo and subsequent Sponsor Girls shows throughout the Southwest was the beginning of barrel racing. The rodeo promoters set up barrels and the women were judged on "horsemanship, on how well they are appointed, their saddles, and how cute they are," said Laegreid. The sponsor contest turned out extremely successful, and all over the country rodeos began to copy the event.

In 1942 the Madison Square Garden Rodeo replaced the cowgirl bronc riders with this new racing "contest." The event, which features running a cloverleaf pattern around three barrels, was the beginning of barrel racing's acceptance on the professional rodeo circuit. (In 1935 the pattern had been changed from the figure eight to a cloverleaf pattern, but was not judged by time until 1949.) It now is the only contest available for women on the national circuit.

LeCompte's observation:

Autry came in . . . and promised short patriotic rodeos. And short means you have to cut out a bunch of acts. Well, this was the time when the soldier was the hero so the cowboy is going to be the hero and the cowgirl is going to be effectively a cheerleader. . . . He put them into parades and square dances on horseback and his rodeos ended up with the Cavalcade of Men Who Made America Great. Flags came tumbling down, speeches were made and you saw people dressed like Abe Lincoln and George Washington and there's no room for women in that story.

After twenty-seven years the West was writing a eulogy for the rodeo cowgirl. The sport once shared by both men and women had reduced women's roles to a beauty pageant on horseback.

Despite these new obstacles the 1930s created, the intrepid Montana cowgirls continued not only to ride whenever they could but also to win national and international titles. Neither RAA rules nor finances nor death could stop them.

Marie Gibson won her second world championship title at Madison Square Garden in 1931. The Greenough sisters had just started their long and illustrious career in 1929. Alice Greenough won the women's world championship in Boston in 1933, 1935, and 1936 and in Madison Square Garden in 1940. They all enjoyed the accolades of 1920s and 1930s crowds in Eastern cities as their careers grew, and they became nationally known as top lady bronc riders.

CHAPTER SEVEN

The Rodeo Life

"The Wild Bunch"

"Rodeo was a different world when Margie and my brothers and I competed. . . .We came from a great era. We called ourselves the Wild Bunch," Alice Greenough wrote for *Persimmon Hill* magazine in 1982. "Rodeo boys were wild and tough, I'll tell you that. Those boys were ranch boys. I mean they didn't sack groceries at a grocery store and go to Little Britches rodeos. . . . Our boys learned the hard way, because they had to."

And the girls did too. "We rode to school, we learned to drive teams, learned to handle horses. . . . It was a good teaching, a good background."

At age fourteen, Alice dropped out of school and took over her dad's mail route. She was the only girl to get a government contract to deliver the mail thirty-seven rural miles out of Billings on horseback. During her first winter Montana suffered record lows—fifty-five below zero at times. She checked out of the post office at eight every morning and sometimes didn't get back until two the next morning. She did the job for three winters and was earning $155 a month when she quit.

Alice made her first appearance at the Madison Square Garden Rodeo in 1929 but couldn't participate in 1930. When a bronc threw

Margie Greenough and Alice Greenough with Ed Lane (one of Teddy Roosevelt's Rough Riders) FROM MARGIE GREENOUGH COLLECTION, COURTESY OF LEIGH ANN BILLINGSLEY

her in El Paso that year, her foot hung up in the stirrup, and "I was drug all the way across the arena." She broke her ankle badly, so bad the doctors considered amputating. "I lay in the hospital there for about nine months," she wrote. "The bones wouldn't calcify." But finally a German doctor came along and pinned her bones with ivory pegs, and her ankle healed.

"I was called 'The Girl with the Ivory Ankle,'" she said. After that, "I wore a boot-shoe, and rode broncs for years that way. It's hard to tell how many head of bucking horses I rode after I had that serious accident."

That was the only time she was in the hospital more than overnight with an injury, and then only when she was carried there unconscious.

Alice was back in New York in 1931, but her foot wasn't yet in shape, although she rode in the "Grand Entry."

Then, in Fort Worth, Texas, in 1932, "an impresario [promoter] from Spain came looking at some of the cowboys and cowgirls. He picked me out to go to Spain." Alice was to ride steers as a curtain raiser to bullfights.

The contract was written in Spanish, and when she arrived Alice found out she was to ride fighting bulls. She might have had second thoughts, since she had understood the word *toro* to mean steers, but "I was never afraid of anythin'. I'm there already—might as well try it."

In her first attempt, the bull burst out of his pen, kicking all four sides into splinters and sending Alice and the attendants flying. "Next time I make sure I get the riggin' on him quick," she said. And it worked.

The only way she could get off after her act was to wait until the bull lunged near the boards, signal the matadors to throw their red capes over his head, then leap for her life.

Alice was one of only a half-dozen men and women to attempt to ride fighting bulls, and the only one to succeed, being thrown only three times, according to an article in the *New York Woman*, reprinted by the *Carbon County News* in January 1937.

And it all happened by mistake.

Interviewed by Teresa Jordan in an article in *Persimmon Hill* magazine in 1982, Alice said,

> *It was unusual to see a girl alone in Spain.... One morning I was walking around with my pants on ... going out to work my trick-riding horse. I came across a whole group of little girls going to school. ... When the girls saw me, the Sisters [their nun teachers] made them turn around and cover up their faces. They weren't supposed to look at me 'cause I had pants on. Course, the little girls giggled and peeked through their fingers. They wanted to see me anyway.*

In 1933 she made a miraculous comeback from that 1930 injury to win her first world championship in Boston, which she would repeat in 1935 and 1936. In that Boston arena Alice and her brother Turk were "the only brother and sister to win world titles in one show," she said later, "both for bronc riding."

"Marge and I worked in every state in the Union but three—Maine, Vermont and New Jersey. They just didn't have rodeos then. It's hard telling how many shows we won."

And every year they would return to Red Lodge for the annual rodeo. "Odds are ten to one [a] Greenough [sister] will win, place, or show in the World's Championship Bronc-Riding Contest for Cowgirls," the *New York Woman* magazine reported.

Miles City held a rodeo called the Range Riders Roundup, wrote Ernest Tooke in *The Montana Cowboy*. During the 1930s Alice was scheduled to ride an exhibition saddle bronc at each of the three performances. "Her first horse didn't do a very good job of bucking, and her second horse ran off." After the day's performances, the cowboys and fans all headed for the nearest saloon.

One man leaned back against the bar and said he didn't think Alice Greenough was much of a bronc rider, a remark that nearly ended in a free-for-all. The next morning, Tooke wrote, his dad (who provided rodeo stock) told his brother Red, "Cut out that bald-faced sorrel that we talked about for Alice."

Red and the other cowmen looked out over the pen, which held three bald-faced sorrels. "Which one?" someone asked. Red pointed to one, and they brought him in for Alice to ride.

"The horse exploded out of the chute as if he had been sitting on a keg of blasting powder," Tooke wrote. "This was no ordinary run-of-the-mill bucking horse. . . . The horse sucked back, sunfished, turned back, and tried to kick the stars out of the sky. He threw everything he had at Alice, but when the whistle blew, she was still sitting in the saddle.

"Red was hopping around, giggling and slapping people on their backs. Dad came running over to Red, and Dad's face was white as a sheet. 'Red!' he said, 'How could you make such a mistake. That was one of the final horses!'"

Tooke concluded, "Dad had saved his five best saddle broncs for the final ride, so the bald-faced sorrel was probably capable of throwing the horn off the saddle. On that day in Miles City, the people saw why Alice Greenough was considered to be the World Champion Lady Bronc Rider."

In addition to bronc riding, Alice was also a flamboyant trick rider and rode in relay races and quadrilles (square dance on horseback).

Described as a tall, graceful woman who wore big black Stetsons, large flapping chaps, and satin shirts, Alice was quick to express her opinion and wouldn't take "no" for an answer. She was described in a newspaper article as "a single-minded woman full of wanderlust . . . hellbent for adventure."

Margaret "Margie" Greenough, on the other hand, was soft-spoken and quiet, not nearly as flamboyant as her sister. Younger by six years, she was also a champion bronc rider.

"No Greenough kid was afraid of a horse," Margie said. "We didn't have sense enough to know we could be seriously hurt. Fear went over our heads like Gene Autry bullets." The Greenough kids learned to ride well out of necessity in their rock-strewn corral at their base camp in the Beartooth Mountains. "Nobody could get bucked off in those rocks and live," Margie said.

But injuries were plenty—broken legs, broken ribs—and once Margie broke her wrist in the chute, waiting to go on. "I switched hands and used that hand from then on."

Despite the rough and tumble life of rodeo, she said of the cowboys they met along the way, "They were gentlemen. . . . If anyone was cussing or talking dirty, they'd tell 'em to hush. And if they didn't, they'd punch 'em." One of those rodeo cowboys would turn out to be husband material.

While riding with King's Wild West Show, Margie met Charles "Heavy" Henson, who bulldogged and rode exhibition broncs in the show. "He was a great big fellow," as Margie described him, a former soldier in World War I who enlisted at age fourteen, a logger, and a bronc rider in Cuba until he broke a leg.

Soon after they met, a bronc fell on Heavy and put him in the hospital. The show moved on, but Margie couldn't get him off her mind.

Alice and Margie Greenough apply lipstick at Madison Square Garden 1938.
FROM MARGIE GREENOUGH COLLECTION, COURTESY OF LEIGH ANN BILLINGSLEY

She went back to watch over him while he mended. They were married not long after that and left the show to follow the circuit on their own.

"There were big contests all over . . . lots of girls riding the broncs," Margie told the *Arizona Daily Star* in September 1994. A baby slowed her down only slightly. She continued riding broncs in the fall of 1930, and Chuck was born in February 1931. "His crib was a pillow in an apple box. He went everywhere with us." Except during her eight-second rides. "One of the cowboys would hold him for me."

The Hensons joined the 101 Ranch Show, and Margie rode as a jockey, rode bareback and saddle broncs, stags (older bulls that had been castrated), and later even rode Brahma bulls. She had started saddle bronc riding the second year on the road with King's show.

"Two of the rankest horses I remember were Little Snow, a white horse, and Skunk, a black-and-white paint," Margie said. "They were both small and quick and real stinkers, but they couldn't buck me off. Later, when I joined Leo Cremer's rodeo, rank horses came in bunches. He had the best string of bucking horses."

(Bobby Brooks Kramer also rode twelve years for Leo Cremer, a well-known Montana stock producer. She said of him: "We all rode for Cremer—Mr. Rodeo—he was the best showman and had good horses. We were all riders—no gender—all contesting.")

Once, as the gate opened for Margie's ride, a man poked her bronc with a hotshot. The horse reared over backward and broke her leg. Heavy saw the whole thing, chased the man down, broke his front teeth, and held his head underwater in a nearby stock tank.

Their son, Chuck, was always there when his mom was injured. He claimed it didn't bother him when he was little. "I'd shout, 'That's Margie Greenough, my mama,' every time her name was announced, whether she was on the horse or under him. [But] by the time I was seven or eight I couldn't stand to watch her ride, because I couldn't stand to see her get hurt."

Chuck was bucked off his dad's horse when he was one, and he became part of the family clown act by age five. At seventeen he was coming along nicely as a calf roper, and he would go on to become famous in his own right as a well-known rodeo clown.

The Greenoughs weren't the only women to continue success-ful rodeo careers during the 1940s. Montana cowgirls didn't get the memo that rodeo was dead to women. As the saying goes, "Where there's a will, there's a way."

CHAPTER EIGHT

Intrepid Is Cowgirl's Middle Name

*"Nothing is impossible, the word itself
says 'I'm possible!'"*

—Audrey Hepburn

A small white schoolhouse squatted forlornly in the center of a
dusty sagebrush flat at Valentine, Montana. As eleven-year-old
Jane Burnett Smith and her family approached the school on July 4,
1930, the young girl saw one lone bucking chute tucked away behind
the school. Then the rodeo fans began to arrive, automatically parking
their cars in an oval to form an arena.

Heat already sweltered in the morning air, scented with sagebrush
and horse sweat. As Jane finished a breakfast of hot dog and lem-
onade, she felt a tug on her sleeve. The brother of an acquaintance
from school greeted her. "Hey, why don't we try riding a coupla steers?
They're payin' fifty cents a mount."

Jane hesitated. "I was not all that anxious to take part in the rodeo,
especially after seeing the first two cowboys get bucked off right in
front of the chute," Jane wrote in her memoir, *Hobbled Stirrups*, "but
the prospect of being the only person to make a qualified ride took
precedence over my cowardice, and I agreed to ride at least one steer if
they said it was okay."

With the encouragement of the Burnetts' hired man, Nate, Jane crawled down onto a short, stocky Hereford yearling. "I could feel my shaking knees knocking against the inside of the chute. The steer's hair was soft and curly like the calf-hide rug at the ranch, and when Nate pulled the rope tight with my hands under it, palms facing upwards, I could feel twitching nerves running through the hide like escaping air bubbles. I peeked through the gate poles at the waiting crowd, then took a deep breath and nodded."

The chute gate opened, and at the first glimpse of daylight, the steer exploded into the arena. "I had an eerie sensation of being catapulted backwards over a steep cliff, but there was no mistaking the instant I made contact with that hard-packed gumbo dirt." A noise like a punctured balloon escaped from the would-be cowgirl.

As the rodeo clown rushed up to see if she was all right, Jane grabbed the front of his shirt and gasped, "Did I ride him? Did I? Did I?"

"You bet," he lied, "just like a real little cowhand."

Car horns honked, people applauded and cheered. Despite a mouthful of gumbo, the fact that Jane had been thrown only a few jumps from the chute, did not dampen her enthusiasm. She attempted two more steers, was bucked off both, "but even the huge sum of a dollar and fifty cents was not as exciting to me as the fact that I was actually accepted as a rodeo hand on my very first try."

Jane said in an interview later in life, "I just wanted to be one of the boys. I wanted somebody to admire me, to make a fuss over me. It was an ego thing—something I wasn't getting at home."

A few days later she hitched a ride to the Flat Willow Rodeo, where she made several more rides. Jane was having such a good time, she continued hitchhiking to rodeos. She made several successful rides and earned enough to dream of becoming a professional rodeo rider. "Already that life was beginning to get under my black-and-blue skin."

She subscribed to *Hoofs & Horns* magazine and imagined herself in each picture of the glamorous girls in fringed leather skirts.

Jane had a difficult home life, with her parents prone to go off for days to drinking and gambling parties. But they were adamantly opposed to Jane's rodeo aspirations. For a while she thought perhaps she should consider an alternate profession, but "pool playing offered little future for women except as a hobby. I did think there might be a future in some form of show business, but when I mentioned ballet, Mother objected, saying that toe-dancing would make my legs too muscular! The very fact that I was almost as light on my feet as a buffalo cow was not included in this protest. . . .

"Mother was sweet and gentle, but she never understood me," Jane later related.

Jane did find solace in music, and every winter during school she would acquire some type of used musical instrument, from a harmonica to an accordion, a guitar, or a cornet. But in the spring, when she heard about a rodeo somewhere, the instrument was soon in the pawn shop.

In 1933 Jane graduated high school at age fourteen and that fall was the youngest freshman ever to enroll at Montana State University. "I'm afraid the sororities and college parties did not bring about the desired magical change my mother hoped for," Jane wrote. "I could have worked my way through school had it seemed important enough at the time," but after half a semester, she returned to the ranch.

In the spring of 1934, Jane boarded a bus to Wyoming to help a woman ex–bronc rider break colts, but her dad caught wind of her desertion and sent the sheriff to take her off the bus a few miles out of town. Jane was "banished" to the ranch, but once the calves were branded and the herd moved to summer pasture, there was a short lull before haying season started. The family drove to Billings for a Western celebration, but it was rained out.

As the family ate breakfast at the Stockman's Café before heading home, Jane saw a poster for a rodeo in Red Lodge in two days. "I deliberately kept Clint's [her dad's] head turned away." Later she won a coin toss with him to "hang around for one more day."

Jane caught a ride with a couple of cowboys to Red Lodge, where she met the Greenoughs. She wrote, "When Alice and Margie finished riding their broncs, they stood in front of the chutes, arms crossed, looking extremely regal and aloof as they peered out from under their ten-acre hats (as opposed to ten-gallons such as the one worn by us peons)." Jane said Margie was a "sweet gal," but she was not as complimentary about Alice, saying the champion bronc rider "didn't want any other women to compete with her."

The would-be cowgirl was "as awed by the famous family as everyone else was, so I just trailed around behind them, staring."

The Burnett family moved into Lewistown that winter, and the next summer Jane invented the excuse of going to visit her grandfather on the ranch, but she instead headed for a rodeo in Wolf Point with a girlfriend, a "Romeo-magnet."

"At the rodeo headquarters I began to question my decision to travel this far with no assurance of a job, and . . . the extra responsibility of another mouth to feed (to say nothing of her taste for expensive Scotch whiskey)."

The promoters suggested that Jane might be able to earn a few dollars in their "mount money" bareback riding event. A cowboy explained that there was no actual competition offered, but each saddle bronc rider was required to ride at least one bareback bronc every day for one dollar each. This had been designed to fill out their list of events, but none of them really wanted to participate.

"You oughta find a least one bronc rider, maybe more, who'd be glad to turn his bareback over to you and let you have the money," the cowboy told Jane.

The transactions turned out to be surprisingly easy, and by the time Jane finished talking to the riders, she'd agreed to ride a total of eight broncs during the two-day show. "I leaned against the fence, still somewhat dazed at what I had done as I watched some cowboys shooting craps on a saddle-blanket behind the bucking chutes."

Then she overheard, "Can you imagine them birds thinkin' we'd be stupid enough to ride them chute-fightin' barebacks fer a buck apiece?"

No wonder it had been so easy. She then learned that the promoters had searched the open country for green broncs that had never been inside a corral, much less a bucking chute. Jane began to wonder what she was in for.

Jane Burnett Smith rides a bronc at Elk City, Oklahoma. COURTESY OF CAMILLE SMITH

"The one-woman rodeo I put on . . . was pretty wild," Jane wrote. "I came out of the chute, bucked off, stumbled back, and prepared to mount another bronc." She stayed until the end of the day and collected her four-dollar pay.

The next day, Jane was back for four more rides. "I crawled down on a big black chute-fighting bronc that had his ears laid back, waiting for me. His powerful muscles were quivering so much it was almost impossible for me to grip the surcingle. Or maybe it was not the horse that was shaking. After all, why in hell would he be afraid?"

The gate flew open and "it was immediately evident the black horse was not scared, even one little bit. He tossed me what felt like

83

eighty-two feet, six and three-eighths inches into the air. The ground jumped up and caught me with a loud thud. I did not care much whether I got up or not."

Seventeen-year-old Jane lay there, aching all over, "wishing bronc riders were allowed to cry."

Despite the pain and bruises and humiliation, she continued to travel to rodeos, looking for bronc-riding jobs.

Traveling to Sheridan, Wyoming, Jane met a major obstacle. The rodeo promoter, a thin-faced man with high cheekbones and bright blue eyes, told her, "Sorry, little lady. We don't hire no women bronc riders."

Jane was taken aback, but before she could protest, he added, "But I've got a job fer you if you can ride relay."

"You bet," Jane replied. "Just so I can try out the horses first." Meanwhile she was hoping he would give a clue what was expected in a relay race. She'd never done it and had paid little attention to those events at other rodeos, being more concerned with the steer and bronc riding.

"Come with me, little lady," the promoter, Barney, said. "We'll bring the horses out on the track right away. You won't need to change saddles, like they do in the men's relay—but then you know all that."

"Yeah." Jane nodded weakly. She was just about to admit she would never be able to get on those tall horses in a hurry, when Barney came to her rescue.

"C'mon, I'll give you a leg up, then when you've gone around once, I'll holler to let you know when it's time to start gettin' off. The horse'll pull into the next station by hisself and I'll be there to catch him and give you a leg up on the next one. Okay?"

Jane nodded again. Her mouth was too dry to speak. Up she went, Barney shouted, "Go!" and the horse took off.

"The wind and fear made my eyes water. My hair was streaming behind me," Jane wrote. "I kept praying the horse knew what we were doing because I was numb. In what seemed like a fraction of a second, we had completed our first lap and I heard Barney shouting, 'Start gettin' down!'"

Jane looked over the point of the big bay's shoulder and saw the ground flying past. No way was she getting off at that speed. While Barney kept yelling, "Get down!" she made another loop of the track.

As they approached the stands the second time, Barney gave an ultimatum. "You get down off'n that horse right now, or so help me I'll shoot you off!"

That gave Jane the incentive and courage to try. With her left foot still in the stirrup, she swung her right leg over and squatted on the horse's side. Lo and behold, the bay began to pull over. "For the first time I felt some confidence. This was what the horse was trained to do."

Then her foot slipped out of the left stirrup, and she was dragged across the dusty track until Barney caught the reins.

She was fired.

Back in Montana a few weeks later, she heard of a small one-day rodeo in an arena in the foothills near Lewistown. Jane caught a ride into town, located the promoter in a back booth at the Montana Tavern, and asked to participate, prepared with a list of her accomplishments to counter his objections.

"Sure," he replied without looking up from some papers. "But you'll have to ride saddle broncs. I don't like to see you little gals trying to ride barebacks and steers."

Ecstatic, Jane looked through the bars, finding a cowboy to take her out to the rodeo grounds. "Do you have your own hobbles and reins?" he asked.

"Hobbles?" Jane was taken aback. "The only hobbles I own are the ones I put on my saddlehorse when I let him graze."

After the cowboy stopped laughing, he took her to a saddle shop for her gear. He held the leather straps outstretched and explained, "See how there's a loop at each end when they're buckled? Have somebody fasten one end through a stirrup on the far side . . . then bring the hobbles under his belly and buckle the other end into the stirrup on your side."

"But why? How can you spur a horse with your stirrups tied down?" Jane asked, puzzled.

"Women bronc riders don't have to spur, kid. Didn't you know that? The idea is to make it possible for you to ride a rougher bronc . . . 'cause if your stirrups stay down next to his belly, all you gotta do is keep your feet in the stirrups and you got 'er made in the shade."

Jane squirmed down into the saddle, and the cowboy handed her the reins (women were allowed two, while men rode with only one). "I tried to wiggle even deeper into the saddle. I shoved both feet into the stirrups and turned my toes outward. I had to get out of there fast. They waited for me to nod . . . the clue to open the gate. They waited. I froze."

"You like rodeoin', kid?" the cowboy asked.

Jane nodded. That was the signal they needed. The gate swung open, and the roan lunged into the arena, bucking fast and kicking high. For the first few jumps, Jane flopped from the cantle to the swells of the saddle with no control. "Then a kind of rhythm seemed to take over, where my body was in kind of a rocking motion as he lunged and kicked. . . . I was actually riding!"

The pickup man rode up to help her off. He grabbed for the rein, but Jane kept jerking it out of his reach. "Damn it, Tony, leave me alone," she yelled. "I found a horse I can ride, and I'm not gonna get off."

Jane's saddle bronc riding career was launched, and she traveled the country, riding for mount money or arranging a "hat collection" for her performances. She was hooked.

Her ventures were not always successful. Once when she was sixteen, she rode to Lewistown and treated herself to a new silver satin shirt and black gabardine pants, hoping she might be chosen rodeo queen. She was not. That disappointment was topped by the promoter forbidding her to ride because she was too young. "You haven't any business riding broncs as tough as these. Not yet, anyway."

Jane was too flabbergasted to tell him about all the steers and broncs—bareback and saddle—she'd already ridden since she was eleven.

Rodeo meant finding her niche in life "where I was accepted as one of the 'hands' and made me feel like I finally belonged somewhere," she said. Her rodeo career would take her all across the United States and into Mexico. "Rodeo people took such good care of me. They helped me rather than take advantage of me. I never felt like 'the kid.'"

But she was also to get "in and out of fights, hospitals, jails and marriages; get whipped in several different states, bucked off in a few of them and divorced in a couple of others. All because I had 'hired out for a tough hand' and thought I had to follow through without complaining."

The road was a bumpy one for rodeo riders, sometimes sleeping six to a bed, wondering where the next dollar for food was coming from. But, Jane wrote, "No matter how broke I was, or what experiences I had in or out of the arena, I held on even tighter, just hoping the next rodeo would be the good one—where I'd ride a tough bronc, make a lot of money, and finally be accepted as a 'top hand.'"

There was always that inner craving for excitement, despite the hardships and the danger. Danger is a matter of perspective, as Jane told of being terrified watching three women in a tight-rope act high above the arena without a net. But while she waited her turn to ride a bronc, the women approached her and asked why she did this dangerous thing—they were so frightened for her.

"You're afraid for me?" Jane was shocked. "Ladies, I wouldn't trade jobs with you for all the beer in Milwaukee!"

In *Hobbled Stirrups* she explained her feelings about riding:

On many occasions you lie awake the night before a rodeo and imagine each phase of easing down onto your bronc, taking your rein, and putting your feet into the stirrups. Your mouth gets dry and the fear is so real that the knots in your stomach muscles draw your knees right up under your chin.

And yet, oddly enough, when you get to the rodeo and your stock actually comes into the chute, you begin getting ready for your ride and feel more like you were looking through a telescope and watching someone else perform miles away from where you are.

I think most riders feel amazingly calm during this period but there is a kind of delayed reaction that does not take over until your ride is complete. Some riders' hands will shake, their lips begin to quiver, and nearly all of them want to talk, talk, talk—preferably about the ride they just completed, but any subject will do. There are others who don't want anyone to come near them until they have had a chance to return to normal. The physical strain is minor compared to the emotional stress.

I was always one of the "chatterers" both before and after a ride.

CHAPTER NINE

The Germ of a Dream

"Where there is no struggle, there is no strength."
—OPRAH WINFREY

While Jane Burnett did run into a couple of rodeo promoters who wouldn't let her ride, Montana rodeos were not yet joining the ranks of the RAA in prohibiting women from riding rough stock, to the Brander sisters' advantage.

THRONGS VISIT THE CITY FOR LABOR DAY DOINGS
First annual Roundup is Huge Success
The riding of the Brander sisters, Margaret and Violet, of Deer Lodge,
proved to be one of the star attractions of the big show. The girls rode
the bucking horses and steers and took part in the races and contests,
winning the wild cow milking event Monday, and other contests.
—Silver State Post, Deer Lodge, Sept. 4, 1930.

The Brander sisters continued their rodeo career in the 1930s, despite the Western states' trend of banning women's competition. The family had also hit hard times during the Depression, and their father had to sell not only his homestead but all of his logging equipment, horses, and sawmills to pay of his debts. Vi, Marg, and the older brothers assumed the responsibility of supporting the family.

They moved to a ranch for sale by the US government at a low price near St. Ignatius. This piece of land proved worthless, but during the short time they lived there, the Brander sisters ferried their horses across Flathead Lake and rode the twenty miles to Kalispell to take part in rodeos.

But Vi and Marg had the germ of a dream—to start a dude ranch and promote their own rodeos. Traveling to rodeos was a hard, rough life, and the shows had begun to lose their allure. To gain experience in dude ranching, they moved to Butte and applied for jobs.

A reporter, Dick Evans, heard of their search for work and wrote an article about their quest: "'We've tried most every kind of ranching there is except dude ranching; we've wrangled most every kind of animal except hogs—now we're looking for a chance to learn dude ranch and pretty soon we hope to have our own ranch,' thus spoke Misses Violet and Margaret Brander, 'branders' in act as well as in name, cow punchers, horse wranglers, bronco twisters, sheep shearers and steer riders. . . ."

Finally, after several years, Vi and Marg had enough money to start their dream ranch, leasing a 640-acre place four miles east of Avon for ninety dollars a year. They called it the Circle Star Ranch, for their registered brand.

A picture-perfect acreage, it featured rock walls that climbed above the tumbling waters of Dog Creek and its borders of willow, lodgepole and yellow pine, and firs. Deep still pools offered prime trout fishing spots for visitors, and sightings of bobcat, bear, coyotes, and deer were common in the wilderness.

The Brander sisters' experience helping in the logging industry paid off. Three of their younger sisters, Alice, (Helen) Kay, and June, joined them, and they immediately went to work getting logs to build three cabins and a ranch house. Kay and June, in their early teens, were guides for their guests through the mountains, and when the dudes were ready to go back home, Vi drove them to the train station Old West style, in a stagecoach pulled by a team of jet black horses. The other sisters galloped alongside, whooping and occasionally firing shots into the air, faking a robbery to entertain the Easterners.

The next building project was an arena, bucking chutes, and corrals so they could stage their first rodeo in 1931. Again the five sisters cut posts and poles, dug holes, nailed on top and bottom rails, and strung woven wire in between.

Riders from all over Montana and as far away as Arizona came to compete and help with chute work. Although none of the Brander boys ever rodeoed, all six sisters took part.

The sisters, dressed alike—in white shirts and pants, or blue sweaters with black trousers, or white shirts with red pants—put on a quadrille, or square dance, on horseback with cowboy partners. This entertaining event was a favorite of their audiences and took many hours of practice.

Vi put on a performance on her saddle horse Mickey, who pranced around the arena on her hind legs, and a bucking exhibition with her never-fail horse Goldy.

Vi and Marg rode broncs, and the other girls rode white-faced steers with a surcingle as their only handhold. Even ten-year-old Florence rode calves.

"We put on a rodeo as something for dudes to enjoy," Marg said. "It was something different—women doing it all."

The Circle Star rodeos went on for five years, helping to pay the lease. The life of a cowgirl wasn't all glamour and romance. Although the rodeos themselves were fun, the preparation was difficult work. The sisters had to round up the animals for the event a few days ahead of each show. They rode all day, sometimes in heavy lightning and thunderstorms in pouring rain, other days scorched by the sun and their breathing stifled by the dust.

Helen Kay wrote in *Let 'er Buck*, "It was hard, sweaty, backbreaking work from sunup until midnight every day if need be until the day of the rodeo. Then, somehow, the romance of it all came through and everything fell into place. The excitement, the crowds, the dusty arena and smell of hot dogs and hamburgers blurred the memory of getting ready and the thought that once the rodeo ended, the stock had to be taken back to (the) ranges. . . ."

Each rodeo was followed by a dance at the hall the Brander sisters had built themselves. Again they felled lodgepole pine, limbed out the logs, peeled them, and hauled them with a team of horses to the site. The girls built the dance hall, pole by pole; put on the roof; and laid the hardwood floor—all themselves.

In August 1933 Vi married Oscar "Pal" Beebe, a cowboy she'd met during her earlier rodeo career. They moved into one of the cabins, and four years later Marlin Dale was born. Vi rode horseback and did her routine work, wearing bib overalls to hide her matronly shape, almost up to the day her son was born.

Helen Kay wrote that her sister kept the secret from all of them until close to the date of the birth. Then one evening Kay "walked over to Vi, whacked her smartly on the abdomen" and asked, "What've you got in there anyhow?" Vi just laughed, still not revealing her condition.

CHAPTER TEN

The 1940s Bring Showmanship

*"I would spin four ropes at one time, one in each
hand, one with my foot, one with my mouth."*
—TRIXI McCORMICK

A s the war situation in Europe worsened in the 1940s, rodeo stock grew scarce and transportation resources were limited. Rodeo producers found it difficult to maintain their rough-stock strings, and there were only fifteen to twenty professional women riders nationally, so their events suffered.

"In 1941 was the last year they had girls' saddle-bronc riding in New York," Alice Greenough told the *Red Lodge Weekly*. "After that a few rodeos had exhibition ladies bronc riding, but that about ended the competitive era for women."

However, Montana cowgirls Trixi McCormick and Birdie Askin excelled in trick roping and riding during this time. Trick riding had been featured in rodeos and at fairs for many years by both men and women performing stunts, such as standing upright on a galloping horse. Other stunts included hanging upside down off the side of the horse while attached to a strap or jumping on and off a galloping horse, twirling a rope while hanging parallel to the ground, and even swinging under the belly of the running horse and coming up on the other side.

Trick riding originated as a war weapon for the Russian Cossacks in the late eighteenth and early nineteenth centuries. When Communism overtook Russia, the Cossacks were forced to leave the country, and many moved to America, where they used their talents to earn a living. Their riding provided entertainment, and soon Americans started imitating them. Trick riding became a rodeo event, where the hardest tricks earned the most points.

Trick roping evolved from ranch work, where cowboys spun and threw ropes to catch animals. Over time they developed tricks to show off their prowess, which evolved into competition and became a form of entertainment first known through the Wild West shows.

Women trick riders of history included the Greenough sisters, the Brander sisters, Daisy Parsons, and Marie Gibson of Montana; Vera McGinnis of California; Tillie Baldwin, who emigrated from Norway to New York; Tad Lucas of Nebraska; Prairie Rose Henderson of Wyoming; and Fox Hastings of California.

Florence LaDue, rodeo promoter Guy Weadick's wife, beat World Champion Lucille Muhall in the trick-riding event at the 1912 Calgary Stampede.

At the 1919 Calgary Stampede, Montanan Daisy Parsons, rather than holding an American flag, stood upright on the horse with both arms stretched out. She also did a "Russian drag," a stunt where she hung on to the horse with one foot while dangling inches above the ground.

Ten-time World Champion Cowgirl Trick Rider Florence Randolph of Georgia was the first and only woman to master turning a backward somersault from one horse to another. Florence weighed a mere ninety pounds and was only four feet, six inches tall. Vera McGinnis's (California) most famous trick was the under-the-belly crawl at full speed. Tad Lucas had her right forearm crushed in the 1933 Chicago show when she executed her famous under-the-belly trick and became caught in the rigging. Her horse stepped on her arm and kicked her, and she nearly lost the arm. But a year later she was back, riding with a cast.

William Leonard Stroud of Texas, the 1918 champion, became famous as a trick rider, frequently participating in "Roman Race," standing astride two horses as they galloped around the arena. Many women emulated him, including Montana's Vi Brander and Margie Greenough.

Actor Will Rogers, known for his roles as a cowboy, was an expert trick roper and also served as a role model for several women over the years.

"Do it with style and a smile" was the motto of Connie Griffith of Nebraska. This could have been the Montana cowgirls' theme as well.

⚊ ⚊

The audience ducked as the performer—just five feet, two inches tall and 108 pounds—twirled a seventy-five-foot fluorescent rope over their heads. But her muscular arm never faltered as she strutted across the stage in a beaded buckskin bra, fringed shorts, white Stetson and boots, and silver-conchaed gauntlets. Then she added three more ropes and whistled for her dog, Cutie, who came out also spinning a small rope.

Trixi McCormick was born Eithel Stokes in Grinder, Missouri, but her parents later moved the family to Hamilton, Montana, where her rancher father, Jody, became Ravalli County sheriff. She grew up riding with her dad—an expert horseman himself—and using a rope every day.

Riding the range under the spectacular peaks of the Bitterroot Mountains, young Eithel fantasized about what kind of world existed beyond those mountains. Even though she loved riding and living on her dad's ranch, she had the urge to see and experience more.

As a teenager she met Bob Rooker, a local cowboy, old-time rodeo producer, and trick-rope artist. She was in awe of his skills and begged him to give her lessons. He taught her some basic rope tricks and "how to smile while performing," and she caught on quickly.

"You have a natural flair for it," Rooker told her. "There aren't many women trick ropers. You could have a great career in rodeo, on stage and in hotel vaudeville. Why don't you give it a try?"

He helped her develop an act, and she performed at county fairs and rodeos, all the while "practicing, practicing, practicing, and adding more tricks," according to her granddaughter Kay McGregor.

Trixi later told Tom Bryant in an interview with *Western Horseman* magazine in 1990, "I learned trick roping by hard work. . . . I worked many, many, many hours every day on rope twirling. Then I started putting tricks in."

She expanded her repertoire, even adding tap dancing and playing the harmonica while spinning. "Back before television, rodeos were major entertainment," she said. "People came to rodeos to see a show, and I put on one for them."

Eithel was married in her early twenties, and they lived high on a mountain near Ovando. In about 1934 her husband stole her trick saddle and left. "She walked out of there in the middle of winter with her two little kids [Jack and Jerry]," related McGregor. "She had a tough character."

Trixi later lamented, "I wish I could have been a better mother to my two children. But I did the best I could. When I got married, he and I both were about the mental age of twelve. Just kids trying to raise kids, a ready-made recipe for disaster."

Now that she had children to raise on her own, she worked to perfect her talent at trick roping and riding.

"I was just a country kid and didn't know acting from sic 'em, but I listened and learned and kept practicing," she told *Western Horseman* magazine.

She won a spot in a Wild West show, and she was off to see the world and prove what a Montana cowgirl could do. Unfortunately the show folded after a few weeks and left her stranded in Detroit, with nothing but her ropes and a harmonica. Noticing that nightclubs were booking specialty acts, she got an audition with an agent—"in my run-down boots, jeans, and hat."

The agent watched her perform and asked, "Do you perform in that?"

With a certain amount of embarrassment and trepidation, she told him that she did.

He shook his head. "Your figure is stunning. You might have a better chance if you change your costume."

The agent then encouraged her to adopt a "short wardrobe," an abbreviated skirt and skimpy top.

"I'd never heard of such a thing," she said, but she went along with his suggestion, which did make her rope-trick performances easier. She was one of the first rodeo women to wear fringed buckskin shorts, a beaded buckskin bra, white boots, and silver-concha gauntlets in the arena.

The agent also decided Eithel wasn't really catchy as a stage name. "'Trixi' sounds good," he told her, and because she'd been married to a man with the last name McCormick, she went by that name from then on, even changing it legally.

Trixi later made her own costumes, which were considered a bit scandalous, since they showed her knees, legs, and a bare midriff.

At a Guy Weadick Stampede in Calgary one year, Trixi performed in tights and a skimpy halter top. "Sure enough, people were screaming the Cowgirl from Montana was riding nude," an Ovando neighbor, Howard Copenhaver related. "It made all the papers in the East. And it sure enough put Calgary on the map."

But the trick-roping cowgirl was not one to be put down by criticism. Once, while riding in Omak, Washington, she was wearing skintight pink pants. "I started into the hippodrome stand—feet in harness, body arched, reaching for the sky—when my trousers split in the rear. The show had to go on, so I filled in the rest of my act with stunts requiring less 'back exposure.'"

The cowboys teased her afterward, saying she "looked like a white tail deer bounding down the arena."

"My act really began to take on excellent dimensions when I found the perfect horse, an Arabian gelding I called Silver Dollar," Trixi told a writer from the *Great Falls Tribune* in 1971. The well-trained palomino added to her glamour and exhibited almost human intelligence. He was calm and "housebroken," and Trixi was able to take him into hotel ballrooms or barrooms, elevator lifts, nightclubs, and theaters.

Collage of Trixie McCormick, Montana trick roper and rider COURTESY OF THE OVANDO
HISTORICAL SOCIETY

She used the gentle, well-mannered palomino as a part of her act until
he was twenty-three.

The horse would always stand quietly wherever they performed—
in a rodeo arena or on stage—with a big spotlight focused on Trixi
standing in the saddle spinning her ropes. During her twenty years
and thousands of miles on the circuit, she owned five trick horses, but
Silver Dollar was her favorite.

One of her horses, another palomino named Buddy, apparently
wasn't quite as housebroken. "Once when I was performing in a plush
theatre in Canada, the M.C. was narrating my act," Trixi told *Hoofs
& Horns* magazine. "At one appointed time in the script, he asked,
'What do you do when you want to go home?' Buddy was supposed
to push me and propel me along 'home.' Instead, the palomino picked

that particular moment to go to the bathroom. I was mortified, but the audience laughed heartily."

When asked about traveling the circuit alone, she said, "I was never alone. I had my horse and my dog. My trailer was divided in half, my horse in one half and my dog and me in the other. In the summer we hit the rodeos and fairs and in the winters, hotels and nightclubs."

Building on the basics Rooker taught her, Trixi began to develop a critically acclaimed showmanship. She was one of the first rodeo performers to use fluorescent ropes and costumes.

When a nightclub was too small to accommodate her horse, she performed her acts on a unicycle. "Sometimes I'd spin two ropes, play the harmonica and tap dance at the same time," she recalled. "I sometimes did a takeoff of Will Rogers."

Another act that thrilled audiences was when Trixi dressed in an Indian costume, complete with an authentic war bonnet. "We would do 'End of the Trail' at the climax, with the orchestra playing the 'Indian Love Call,'" she said. "It often made a good night club finale."

One advertisement in the Cass City, Michigan, *Chronicle*, invited the public to a "Big Free Family Party, Monday January 22 [1951], with top talent in a New and Different Entertainment Program. No sales talk, just entertainment." Receiving top billing was "Trixie McCormick, novelty rope and unicycle act."

"I always performed to music, and Silver Dollar seemed to enjoy a rodeo band. I met the 'greats' in rodeo and show business," she told the *Great Falls Tribune*.

Trixi performed in nearly every state in the United States, in Canada, and in Mexico. She traveled coast to coast with Ken Maynard's Western Review, and during that time performed with fan dancer Sally Rand (who was married to Turk Greenough, brother of Alice and Margie), Johnny Mack Brown, Gene Autry, and Rudy Vallee. She also rode with the Lindermans and Greenoughs, Paddy Ryan, Bob Askin, Ray Maverty, and other Montana rodeo personalities.

In late 1939, Jasbo, a cowboy clown and friend, told her that a rodeo company was being formed to go to Australia. She applied to

Trixi McCormick on Silver Dollar, doing rope tricks COURTESY OF THE OVANDO HISTORICAL SOCIETY

go along and was booked as a trick rider in the Royal Easter Show in Sydney, Australia, along with famous bronc and trick rider Tad Lucas.

"I was scared to death," she said, "but the gang [rodeo friends] told me not to worry. When my name was announced, they set me on a horse, pushed me over backwards, and said to go to it."

Her debut "drag" ride was featured in a picture on the front page of the *Sydney Herald* the next day. "That was one of the biggest thrills of my life," she said. "There must have been thousands of people there and they were all on their feet yelling and screaming for me. I'll never forget it." This Australian tour launched Trixi's career, with magazine and newspaper articles lauding her success there.

The press apparently couldn't decide what name to use, and she appeared over the years as Tricksy, Trixye, Miss MacCormack, Mrs. Mcormack, Maxine McCormack, Ethel McCormick, and Dixie McCormick. She was also written up as being from Butte, Deer Lodge, Missoula, Hamilton, Havre, Bozeman, and Billings. Papers described her alternately as a Texas cowgirl, a Chicago showgirl, a New York dancer, a Hollywood starlet, and a California cutie.

Tom Bryant wrote in the 1990 *Western Horseman* article, "What probably kept the press confused was that they were not used to dealing with such a dual dynamo. Trixi performed in nightclubs with grace and aplomb and in rodeos with derring-do. She was, and still is, very hard to categorize."

In her twenty years of performing, she had only one "casualty," breaking her right ankle in three places while practicing trick riding in New York. Her horse "suddenly went sidewise and I fell. It took three months for my bones to heal," she related in the newspaper article.

Trixi also had a close call in Caldwell, Idaho.

I was doing the Cossack Drag, which is hanging by one leg sidewise from the saddle, hands and arms hanging almost to the ground. My pinto, Tango, was running straight-away, but for some reason I'll

*never know I pulled up out of the trick just a second before his feet
went out from under him.*

*He fell and could have broken my back had I been in the earlier
position. As it was, neither of us was hurt.*

In the 1950s Trixi toured with the USO in Japan, Okinawa, Korea,
Australia, and the Philippines, performing with many well-known celeb-
rities such as Bob Hope and Slim Pickens. She spent twenty years tour-
ing the country with her horse and dog, performing rope tricks, and was
internationally billed as "Trixi McCormick: the Cowgirl from Montana."

When she was in large cities, Trixi took time out to visit hospitals
and city parks and perform for young people who normally wouldn't
have had the chance to see a cowgirl act.

"She was a great pro," Turk Greenough (brother of Alice and
Margie) told *Hoofs & Horns*. "No other woman could duplicate her
act. Wherever she appeared, she got stellar billing."

Greenough also praised her strength. "Although Trixi presented
the picture of a petite woman, she was well muscled and strong. She
would have to have strength in her arm to spin a 75-foot rope. This she
did, encircling both herself and her horse."

In 1960 Trixi had had enough of traveling, and she bought the
Brand Bar in Ovando, about sixty-five miles north of Missoula, Montana. Later, when Highway 200 bypassed the little town, she established and ran Trixi's Antler Saloon on the hill just above Ovando for
twenty years. She was well known for her Western artifacts, excellent
down-home cooking, and providing clean cabins for hunters, fisher-
men, and other travelers.

"She was a marvelous cook," her neighbor Margaret Copenhaver
said. "Everybody would agree with that." She often held barbecues,
using wagon wheels as giant platters with aluminum foil between the
spokes.

"The rumors that Trixi's was a brothel is not true," granddaughter
Kay related. She explained that the original bar building had been a
brothel in Helena many years before it was moved to Ovando.

Trixi lived in a room in the back of the bar, and Silver Dollar, now also retired, had a stall right next to her. Kay said he would come into the bar, eat popcorn, and drink beer, right along with the patrons.

The favored trick horse was nearly thirty years old and in pain, and one day when he went down and couldn't get up, Trixi was forced to put him down. "A little bit of my heart went with him," she said.

Kay and her sisters, Kerry and Karla, spent summers helping Grandma Trixi at the restaurant/bar. "She taught us how to cook. When I was little, I would stand on a stool to cook hamburgers, then I would have to clean it the right way. Sometimes we'd go camping and she made beer pancakes."

Trixi also taught Kay to bartend when she could see over the bar— at age fourteen. Kay was always close to her grandmother, and her favorite memory of many was the first time they catered together. She also wanted to trick ride like her grandmother.

"I grew up getting bucked off my horse because I wanted him to do tricks," Kay said. Her grandmother did teach her to do some tricks with the rope and riding. "Except for the unicycle. I never did master that."

The former cowgirl remained a formidable character even in her later years. "If a boy even looked at us, she'd lead us out by the hair," Kay said.

Trixi kept a sawed-off baseball bat, along with a wagon-wheel spoke and an old single-action Colt, under the bar, and more than one person witnessed her using these tools on misbehaving customers.

One time, when a group was creating trouble in the bar, Trixi kicked them out. About three o'clock the next morning, she heard a noise. The men were "messing around" with her car parked outside her bedroom window. "She didn't open a window to yell at them or try to get away. She grabbed her 9mm pistol and shot right through the wall," Kay related. "Unfortunately, she shot the engine block" and ruined her car.

Trixi finally retired for good in the early 1980s, sold the bar, and moved back to Hamilton, where she performed with the Back Country

Horseman Saddle Club. She continued to ride in local parades, still spinning her rope at age seventy.

The Montana Cowgirl died at the age of ninety-one on April 6, 2001, in Coalinga, California, where she lived with her son Jack. She was remembered by many friends and neighbors for her generous spirit and hospitality. "She weighed no more than 120 pounds," said Howard Copenhaver, "and ninety pounds [of that] was her heart."

Trixi had instructed her granddaughters what to do when she died, and so the family cooked for two days, preparing macaroni salad, potato salad with dill pickles and black olives, ham and roast beef, rolls, chili, soup, raw vegetables, and chips and dip. A keg of beer rested next to the coffee pot. Visitors were invited to the Drummond Community Hall to celebrate her life and remember her as a grandmother, friend, cook, hostess, saloon keeper, outdoorswoman, character, trick rider and rope spinner, and inspiration.

"She wanted it to be fun," Kay said. "She wanted people to remember her with smiles, not tears. She showed us all that we could follow our dreams, and not forget what we're here for."

Trixi's Antler Saloon and Family Diner is still operated at Ovando by Ray and Cindy Francis, and it features a photo and memento corner dedicated to Trixi. There is also a museum collection of local history and unique antiques from "old-time" Ovando, with many items dedicated to Trixi, run by the Ovando Historical Society in the former Brand Bar building.

CHAPTER ELEVEN

All in the Family

Birdie was "one to ride the river with."
— *Tri-State Livestock News*

As Bob Askin of Ismay prepared to mount a gnarly looking saddle bronc at a rodeo October 23, 1932, someone handed him a telegram, advising him a baby daughter had been born to him and his wife, Helen. Snugging his hat firmly on his head and with a wide grin, the champion bronc rider rode his horse to the finish. Then he sent a telegram home: "Name her Birdie," for her maternal grandmother, Bertha, nicknamed "Birdie." She was one of eight children born to Helen and Bob.

Bob Askin was known by some in Montana as the "Grandaddy of rodeo." He won the 1925 Saddle Bronc Championship at the Pendleton Roundup, was a four-time world champion, and rode some of the toughest horses in the game. He was inducted into the National Cowboy & Western Heritage Museum in 1978.

Following in her father's ranch and rodeo footsteps, young Birdie took her first ride as soon as she could "crawl up a leg and climb on its back" on her own, at about age three. She immediately fell in love, and the family could hardly get her off horseback from that moment on. She became her dad's "right-hand man" while her brothers were away.

Birdie accompanied her dad to rodeos, and after watching a trick riding exhibition, she began to teach herself tricks "out behind the barn, where I couldn't be seen." But her dad saw her and bought her a trick saddle tree. He later took the silver mountings off his prize saddle and put them on hers.

She explained in an interview with Addison Bragg of the *Billings Gazette* that much of the "trick" to trick riding, is the construction of the saddle, which is made without a cantle and swells. It also has a high horn to aid in vaulting from one side to the other, and straps for various foot, toe, and handholds.

Another major component in trick riding is the horse, according to Birdie. "He's got to run straight, and he's got to be calm enough not to shy at things. And for me he had to be fast." She said her horse, Melody, was one of the fastest. "I always felt the faster I rode, the more showy the act was."

The excitement and appeal of rodeo competition drew Birdie in, and her first performance, at age thirteen, was at an Ekalaka rodeo in 1945, where she won her first seventy-five dollars. Later, while still a teen, she did trick and stunt riding for Gene Autry and other rodeo producers in arenas across North America.

Birdie had no concept of danger or fear while doing headstands on a running horse or hanging from the side or rear of a horse, head only inches from the ground. She said she never thought about the danger or felt any fear.

But there was one time, she admitted, she had a close call. "I was working a rodeo for Leo Cremer at Miles City. I guess was about sixteen," she told her interviewer. "I was doing the Cossack Drag— hanging by my toes from the back of the horse at a dead run—when one of my straps broke."

Birdie didn't use a safety strap, which most riders did to pull themselves back up. "I could have gotten a head full of hoofs, and that would've been it, if it hadn't been for Wally McCrae." The rodeo clown caught Birdie's horse and brought it to a stop, all the while other riders

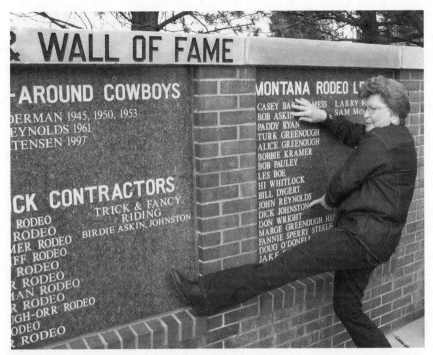

Birdie Askin Johnston points to her, her dad, Bob Askin's, and her husband, Dick Johnson's names on the Montana Wall of Fame. AUTHOR'S COLLECTION

stood by and watched in horror. "I'll never forget Wally for that. He saved my life that day."

Birdie graduated as valedictorian of her high school and attended Eastern Montana College, following her mother's career as a schoolteacher. While still in school she was called back to Ismay to fill in as a temporary teacher, and she stayed through the year.

In Billings Birdie met a young champion bareback bronc rider, Dick Johnston. He left to serve in the Korean War, but after he returned, they were married on November 29, 1952.

"I married a cowboy," Birdie said. They rodeoed together, but she "retired" after they were married. "Dick didn't want me to ride, so I finished out my contract for that season and quit."

Birdie later said she thought she'd gotten out of trick riding at the right time. "It's almost a vanished art now," she admitted in a 1972 interview. Although she had an impressive collection of buckles, ribbons, and cups to show for her career, she also had an equally impressive collection of X-rays on file.

One injury was a broken leg, which happened when she attempted to vault over a running horse in Fort Madison, Iowa. The layoff gave her time to attend Eastern Montana College, she said.

Another performance resulted in a broken arm; her broken toe came from a rodeo at State Line; and she didn't remember where her several broken ribs came from. "The toe hurt worst of all," Birdie said, "but none of them were serious at all."

After retiring from rodeo, and while raising three children during the 1950s, Birdie worked as an ad executive for radio and television, and she ended up hosting a TV talk show. She and Dick also owned the Pack Trail Inn, a popular restaurant in Billings, for many years. Continuing to serve their love of rodeo, they were on the board of directors for the five-state (Wyoming, Montana, Nebraska, and North and South Dakota) Northwest Ranch Cowboys' Association.

In 1969 Dick landed a job as wrangler, teamster, and driver for the filming of the 1970 movie *Little Big Man*, and when he was injured, Birdie stepped in to take over. This role led the Johnstons to a new career, and they moved to Tucson, Arizona, to wrangle horses for many films shot in Arizona, Colorado, and California.

The Hollywood film industry has used southern Arizona since 1925 to provide stunning vistas and charming locales to produce dozens of Westerns and feature films. Film production has been an integral part of Tucson's economic and cultural identity since 1940, the year the film *Arizona* was released. Other well-known movies include *The Bells of St. Mary's*, the 1957 version of *3:10 to Yuma*, *The Last Outpost*, and *The Outlaw-Josey Wales*.

Birdie spent the next thirty years with a wardrobe and makeup trailer, catering to such stars as Ann-Margret, Dean Martin, Burt

Reynolds, Sally Field, Ben Johnson, Steve McQueen, James Garner, Robert Conrad, Richard Pryor, John Candy, Keifer Sutherland, and Tom Cruise.

Also working for television, commercial, and video production companies, she worked with many singers, including Frank Sinatra, Tom Petty, Clint Black, and Kathy Matea.

After the Johnstons were divorced in 1990, Birdie formed a production company and heavy film equipment rental company of her own, and she helped found and serve on the board of directors of the Southern Arizona Film Commission. In between all of her jobs and positions, in 1994 she wrote and produced a music video, "Climb the Ladder," sung by Carol Collins, to commemorate her famous dad.

> "Daddy taught us how to climb the ladder,
> Boy or girl, it didn't matter.
> How to be a hand,
> Not take a back seat to any man.
> Daddy taught the Golden Rule . . ."

Birdie is listed on the Montana Pro Rodeo Hall and Wall of Fame in Billings under "World Champion" for Trick and Fancy Riding; along with her father, Bob Askin, for Saddle Bronc Riding; and her ex-husband, Dick Johnston, for Bareback Bronc Riding. Dick preceded Birdie in death in 2007.

After her death on September, 25, 2010, her obituary in the *Billings Gazette* honored her with these words: "Birdie had a profound effect on folks whose paths she crossed. She worked with and helped people from all walks of life. She was always strong-willed and strong-minded and accomplished her successes her way. She cared deeply for her family and was there for many more than can be told when they needed a hand. Birdie was quiet about these things, and no one ever truly knew the extent of her compassion."

And in the *Tri-State Livestock News*: "Birdie's name is indelibly inscribed on the hearts of all those profoundly touched by her dynamic personality and grace through the years of her life here on earth . . . the multitudes who knew her as 'one to ride the river with.'"

Author's note: I had the great pleasure to meet and share lunch with Birdie Askin Johnston in June 2009. She was a delightful lady, and this was one of the highlights of my Montana book tour, a memory I still cherish.

CHAPTER TWELVE

All-Girls Rodeo

"If you want something done right, do it yourself."
—CHARLES-GUILLAUME ÉTIENNE

Despite the success of many cowgirls in the 1940s, such as Trixi and Birdie, who were able to continue in various ways with their love of rodeo, many were still frustrated by the lack of professional competition on rough stock—like they used to do.

Because of World War II, rodeos all over the country were canceled, many women were forced to take over ranch operations as men went off to war, and the professional cowgirls' role was reduced to beauty pageants with prizes such as cigarette cases.

This next generation of working cowgirls hated the restrictions. They wanted to be judged—like their predecessors—on their riding skills rather than on their beauty and who looked the best in tight pants. Fay Kirkwood, a Texas cowgirl, produced a women's-only exhibition in 1942 to protest against male-dominated rodeos. Women's barrel racing was introduced that same year, at Madison Square Garden's annual rodeo.

Amateur cowgirls in the Southwest began to put on informal all-girl rodeos to provide entertainment for the troops and riding opportunities for themselves.

In September 1947 a group of Texas women produced an all-girl rodeo at Amarillo. Then, after a dispute over rules in an RAA event, thirty-eight women met in February 1948 to form the Girls Rodeo Association (GRA) with its own set of rules.

The GRA was open to cowgirls of all ages and was set up to "organize professional rodeo contestants for their mutual protection and . . . raise the standards of cowgirl contests so they rank among the foremost American sports [and] protect members from any unfair practices on the part of rodeo management."

The first president, Margaret Owens Montgomery, met with the directors of the RCA to include women's contests at the men's sanctioned events. Later, in 1955, Bill Linderman of Montana, RCA's president, signed an official agreement with the organization that women's events at RCA-sanctioned rodeos must also be GRA sanctioned.

That first year saw seventy-six members join GRA, and the organization sanctioned sixty national contests. Titles were awarded in seven categories, including bareback and bull riding, and in 1949 its only saddle bronc title.

All-girl rodeos usually consisted of at least five events, including bareback riding, calf roping, barrel races, ribbon roping, cutting horses, bull riding, wild cow milking, or team roping. Broncs and bulls had to be ridden for six seconds, two reins allowed, and the rider could use hobbles if she wanted to.

Entry fees were ten dollars in each event, and prize money was determined by points. One point was awarded for each dollar won at any approved GRA rodeo that was also an RCA point award rodeo. The All-Around Champion Cowgirl for the year was determined by points won at all-girl rodeos only.

GRA rules were strict about the cowgirls' clothing and area appearance. If they wore jeans, they were to be covered by chaps. Grounds for being banned for the arena included the following:

- Refusing to ride the animal drawn or selected
- Being under the influence of liquor

- Rowdyism
- Mistreatment of stock
- Altercation or quarreling with judges or officials
- Failure to give assistance when requested by the arena director

The GRA opened the door once again for professional female rough-stock riders, but they no longer competed in the same arena and drew from the same stock as the men. However, this organization helped barrel racing—the only sanctioned women's event in the RAA (now PRCA)—evolve to become a standard contest at most major rodeos and today offers purses that compete with the PRCA. The GRA became the Women's Professional Rodeo Association in 1981 and is recognized as one of the world's largest rodeo sanctioning bodies.

After the war, more leisure time revived rodeos' popularity and youngsters became involved on the college level. Needing a sanctioning body, twelve schools met in Texas in 1949 to form the National Intercollegiate Rodeo Association (NIRA). They included women, although the National Finals standings on NIRA's website do not list women's standings until 1956.

Bozeman, Montana, began hosting the college finals in 1973, and that became its home for the next twenty-four years. The sport grew consistently through the years and during the 1960s received a huge boost when the College National Finals Rodeo was televised on ABC's *Wide World of Sports.*

"Preserving Western heritage through collegiate rodeo" has been a theme for more than sixty years, and several professional rodeo stars follow their roots to college rodeo. These riders include Roy Cooper, Chris LeDoux, Ty Murray, Tuff Hedeman, and Dan Mortensen (Montana).

The Collegiate National Finals Rodeo in Casper, Wyoming, is the "Rose Bowl" of college rodeo. The NIRA crowns individual event champions in saddle bronc and bareback riding, bull riding, tie-down roping, steer wrestling, team roping, barrel racing, breakaway roping, and goat tying. National team championships are also awarded to men's and women's teams. More than 400 cowboys and cowgirls from 137 colleges compete each year. Women compete in bareback riding, team roping, barrel racing, breakaway roping, and goat tying.

CHAPTER THIRTEEN

Who Wants to Retire?

*"You're never too old to set another goal or
to dream a new dream."*

—C. S. Lewis

The war years may have forced most cowgirls to retire from competition, but Alice Greenough didn't retire from rodeo. She teamed up in the rodeo business with an old friend and former bull rider, Joe Orr, and they formed the Greenough-Orr Rodeo Company in 1943.

"We started right out with nothing, but every time we'd have a little money we'd buy a bucking horse. We put together a good string of bucking horses and sent them to the [Madison Square] Garden," she told Teresa Jordan in *Cowgirls: Women of the American West.* "After two years of that we decided to keep our own good bucking horses and put on our own shows."

The couple furnished stock for rodeos throughout Idaho, Montana, Wyoming, Canada, the Dakotas, and as far east as Milwaukee. Joe took care of the stock; Alice ran the office, kept the books ("I didn't even have an adding machine the first two years."), ran the arena, and paid the cowboys. And she rode broncs as an exhibition during the shows. The Orrs also offered some of the first women barrel-racing events and featured many nationally known trick riders.

"Birdie Askin, daughter of great cowboy Bob Askin, trick rode at our Montana Rodeos [and] Trixi McCormick, a trick roper and rider . . .," Alice wrote in *Persimmon Hill* magazine in 1974, listing all the cowgirls she'd worked with in her career.

A lot of girls did a man's work—because they had to. Cowboys and ranchers went to world wars, left the women and girls to do the work. . . .

Most of the girls in Rodeo yesterday came in young and stayed a long time, improving with experience. They accepted the hard knocks and long hours of driving with few of the comforts we have today. . . . Rodeo is deluxe today. There are schools to teach anything from barrel racing to bull riding . . . there are fancy house trailers, horse trailers, and campers—but I really don't think it makes better riders or rodeo hands. Some are better athletes than cowboys.

Alice also lauded the women "behind the scenes," including Mae Zumwalt, wife of Missoula-area stock contractor and rodeo producer Oral Zumwalt.

"That rodeo life was a good old life. We were all so close-knit. It's a friendship that we created over the years," she said. "I'm proud and happy to have been among the best, winning my share around the world."

One day in 1958 Joe said to her, "Why don't we get married? You don't know anybody else, and I don't want anybody else."

"Sounds like a good idea," Alice replied. "I've known you all my life. I know all your faults and you know mine."

And so they became partners in marriage as well as in business.

Alice served as rodeo secretary and chute boss for the Miles City Bucking Horse Sale for several years, and the Orrs produced rodeos until 1958, when they sold the business to the Fettig brothers of Killdeer, North Dakota. That year Alice rode her last exhibition bronc in Greybull, Wyoming. But every year she returned to Red Lodge on July 4 for the Home of Champions Rodeo. She rode in her last parade there in 1992.

Alice Greenough riding bronc COWGIRL RODEO PHOTO FILE, AMERICAN HERITAGE CENTER, UNIVER-SITY OF WYOMING

In 1959 Alice established the Carbon County Museum in a log cabin in Red Lodge to house the collection of her world-renowned rodeo family as well as the Linderman rodeo collections. The museum serves as an archive on early ranching and rodeoing in the West.

Later that year the Orrs moved to Tucson, Arizona. After Joe died in 1978, Alice and her sister, Margie, who then lived next door, operated a livestock-exchange restaurant in Tucson. The sisters frequently did stunts and drove wagons for movies and television series about the West, including *Little House on the Prairie* and *Father Murphy*. However, Alice said the movie organizations and guilds did not give her the freedom that rodeo had.

She had first encountered Hollywood when she performed trick riding in the 1937 film *The Californians*. During her career Alice hobnobbed with royalty and American socialites such as Cornelius Vanderbilt, and she became friends with American Heavyweight Boxing Champion Jack Dempsey.

Alice has been credited with teaching Dale Evans, wife of cowboy movie star Roy Rogers, how to ride. She continued working in the Western film scene until she was eighty.

Alice was a colorful and dynamic woman who didn't let anything stand in the way of her rodeo career. At a gathering in 1995 after Alice died at age ninety-three, one friend described her as "bossy. Oh, she was bossy. God himself must be wondering why he asked her to go on her last ride up there."

Sister Margie told the *Arizona Daily Star*, "Alice had her own way of doing things. She got your attention."

Another neighbor said, "She wouldn't take no for an answer. She just got up and did it. She could dance. She could ride. She could hoot 'n' holler. She was a great lady. She had nerves of steel."

"They don't make 'em like that anymore," remarked another. "The whole damn country ain't the same. I reckon just about everything's gone downhill since the days when Alice was queen of the rodeo."

Others said she was generous and hospitable, and she encouraged fallen riders when they were down, gave riders cash when they needed a saddle or a bus ticket home.

Alice's single-mindedness led her to abandon her first husband and children early on to do what she loved best. She married several times, although she claimed in at least one interview that she waited until late in life to marry (Joe Orr).

"Mom was America's first liberated woman," her son E. Jay Franklin Cahill told a newspaper reporter after her death. "I didn't see her for the first seven years of my life. After that she'd sometimes take me out to dinner and buy me a cowboy hat, and then she was gone again." He said he'd see her occasionally when the rodeo came to town or in the movies. "But I didn't hold anything against her. She was what you call a star. In her time, what she did—telling the man to raise the children—was not approved of. With professional women nowadays, it happens all the time. She was a brave one."

"She had one heck of a life," said her nephew, rodeo clown Chuck Henson, Margie's son. "She never smoked or drank, and she was quite the lady." He told the story of how Alice, on her way to her ninety-third birthday party, refused his help and insisted on climbing into his truck by herself. "Hard-headed is what you call it," he said. She even earned the nickname "She-Boss" among her contemporaries.

A lifelong friend, Jim Barrett, described Alice as "a great person. She was a great credit to the ladies—she was on her last saddle bronc when she was fifty-five years old. I figure she'd been on about eighteen hundred bucking horses in her lifetime."

Ernest Tooke of Ekalaka wrote about her in the book *The Montana Cowboy: An Anthology of Western Life*: "I doubt if we'll ever have another lady as versatile around a rodeo as Alice Greenough. I think those of us who had the privilege of knowing this fine lady will feel that she was the 'Queen of the Cowgirls.'"

Great-nephew Deb Greenough, a world champion bareback rider himself, said of Alice, "She was tough. She was a leader in her own way—and she was strong." He told of her coming to him before a rodeo just two years before she died and offering to help adjust his equipment. Deb Greenough retired from rodeoing in 2001.

Alice taught her grandniece Cathy Jo Ledoux "all about horses. But mostly she was a hero to look up to because she was a great woman."

Reporter Paul Brinkley-Rogers wrote in her obituary for the *Arizona Republic*, "Some say the American cowboy hero is myth. But then, to prove skeptics wrong, you have a hard-riding bronc buster like Alice Greenough Orr. . . ."

Alice was one of the first members inducted into the National Cowgirl Hall of Fame in 1975, and Margie followed in 1978. In 1983 they were initiated into the Cowboy Hall of Fame, along with their brother Turk. Nephew Chuck Henson entered in 1995. Alice was also a 2010 Montana Cowboy Hall of Fame Inductee.

Alice Greenough was further honored as Best Woman Athlete by Birth State–Montana as reported by *Sports Illustrated* and CNN. She was also named as one of Montana's one hundred most influential persons in the twentieth century.

Alice Greenough Orr died in August 1995 at the age of ninety-three.

While Alice was the more flamboyant and well known of the Greenough sisters, Margie Greenough Henson was also a champion bronc rider. Born the seventh of eight children in 1908, she began her career by winning a fifteen-dollar purse for a half-mile cowgirl race at the Red Lodge rodeo in 1924. She continued rodeoing through the 1930s and 1940s, until she retired in 1954, sometimes beating her older sister. She often was the only woman bronc rider in the rodeo. She competed seven years at Madison Square Garden and took second place there twice. Margie won her first saddle at Ogden, Utah, in the 1940s and was awarded her prize by the late film star Wallace Beery. She also won the Tri-State bronc riding events for three consecutive years, competing against riders from Arkansas, Missouri, and Oklahoma.

"I competed in rodeos in every state in the nation, with the exception of Maine," she told the *Tucson Daily Citizen* in a 1963 interview. "I never heard of a rodeo in Maine, so never went to compete." This article announced that the Greenough sisters were to ride again—in the Fiesta de los Vaqueros parade.

Margie attributed her success to "a good sense of balance and lots of practice." She and Alice had their share of injuries and broken bones. "Anyone who rides the rodeo for any length of time gets a few broken bones," she said.

Bucking broncs—both bareback and saddle—were the sisters' specialty, and "I've ridden bulls too," Margie said. "But I wasn't a very good bull rider. When it came bull-ridin' time, my heart was just a pounding." Whether bulls or horses, the women rode the same as the men, having their mounts picked from the same stock.

"I enjoyed every bronc I ever been on," she remarked in the documentary *I'll Ride That Horse*. But "the biggest thrill of my life was to ride up out of that basement into the Madison Square Garden arena."

"They were ranch-raised and they had to work for everything they got. Riding in rodeos was one of the easiest ways for them to make money," Margie's son, Chuck, said, "better than they were making working as waitresses in Red Lodge."

Margie Greenough riding a bronc at the Pueblo, Colorado, state fair COURTESY OF DONALD
C. & ELIZABETH M. DICKINSON RESEARCH CENTER AT THE NATIONAL COWBOY & WESTERN HERITAGE MUSEUM

Even by the time the Greenough sisters were in their sixties, they
vowed that, if they were twenty-five years younger, they would follow the rodeo circuit again in a heartbeat. "Despite the town-to-town
travel, the mud, rain, and cold, it was a wonderful life and you lived
with fine people," Margie said.

Claiming that rodeo was born in her, Margie was just as proud
of her son, grandchildren, and great-granddaughter and their rodeo
accomplishments as she was of her own. When Margie died in 2004
at age ninety-six, she was the last of the Riding Greenoughs.

Director Jack Young told *American Cowboy* magazine, "I was
always glad to see Margie and Alice coming. They could hitch and
drive any kind of harness rig, from a buggy to a four-horse team, and
they owned their own vintage costumes."

J. P. S. Brown also wrote in *American Cowboy,*

Everyone who knew Margie and Alice agrees they may have been wild when they performed in the arenas, but they always behaved as ladies. They wore trousers and chaps when they performed, but for formal occasions they donned suits, skirts or dresses, which was the only acceptable behavior of their time. They handled dignitaries and interviewers with good manners and the same poise and aplomb as they handled rough cattle and horses. People who met them outside the arena would never have believed they were tough enough to stomp a bronc, because their speech was as refined as any eastern debutante's and their behavior unsullied. Because of this they were admired and respected by everyone who knew them.

This description could have fit any of the Montana cowgirls.

CHAPTER FOURTEEN

Where Did They End Up?

"I look back on my life like a good day's work, it was done and I feel satisfied with it. I was happy and contented, I knew nothing better and made the best out of what life offered. And life is what we make it, always has been, always will be."

—Grandma Moses

After her husband, Bill, died in 1940, Fannie Sperry Steele continued to run the ranch by herself for another twenty-five years, shoeing and breaking her own horses, guiding hunters into rough country, and carrying cans of fish over treacherous terrain to stock mountain streams.

In 1975, when Fannie was seventy-eight, Bill's son wrote to tell her he'd sold the ranch, and she prepared to move to her sister and brother-in-law's homestead cabin in the Beartooth Mountains. As her greatnephew Dave pulled his truck up to help her move, he brought her a letter postmarked Oklahoma City. Fannie opened the letter and looked at her helpers in astonishment. "I've been chosen a charter life member of the Cowboy Hall of Fame. They remember." She was one of the first women inducted, along with Bertha Blancett, Lucille Mulhall, and Florence Randolph. She was also inducted into the National Cowgirl Hall of Fame in 1978.

At age eighty-seven Fannie reluctantly admitted she could no longer live alone and moved to a retirement home in Helena. She had put off this final move as long as she could. "My greatest worry will be the well-being of my pintos. I can leave the range, since I have had a full share of life on it. I can quit the ranch and ranch house and my souvenirs, but I hate like hell to leave my pintos behind."

At her ninetieth birthday party, Fannie raised a toast: "To the yesterdays that are gone, to the cowboys I used to know, to the bronc busters that rode beside me, to the horses beneath me—sometimes—I take off my hat. I wouldn't have missed one minute of it."

Sheryl Monroe wrote of her great-aunt, "I'll never forget the summer I spent with Aunt Fannie on her dude ranch. It was 1957, a year before I graduated from high school. . . . I admire her so much for being such a strong woman. . . . I'm proud to have known her and the other cowgirls of her day that she encouraged and helped along the way. [They] are surely glad they met my Great Aunt Fannie."

A great-nephew, Walter Jester (Fannie's brother Walter's grandson), related a similar story about riding his first horse at Fannie's ranch when he was a small child and helping put up hay on shares to help feed his family's own horses. "I spent quite a few summers with her. She was a class act, had a great sense of humor, and she taught me a lot about horses."

A neighbor in the Helmville area, Mary Hamilton, related a story told by Tom Geary, one of the county workers who drove the snowplow near the Steele place on Arrastra Creek in the 1950s:

In the winter, the county road crew had a good neighbor policy of plowing everyone's lane when the snow quit for a few days and they got caught up. But the county commissioners discussed the hazard of this service (for which they sent an annual bill) and decided that some cattle guards weren't up to "standards." The first one that had to go was Fannie Steele's.

Verner Bertelson, then county commissioner, was delegated to tell her, and she wasn't a bit pleased. Tom Geary, then county foreman and the person who told me this story, took his pick and shovel to the Steele place and dug the cattle guard out. "She built it herself at the age of sixty. It was all hand hewn, poles laid in snug as could be, there wasn't a nail in it!" Then he said, "If I'd spun out on it with a set of chains on, I might have popped a pole loose, but I doubt it."

I asked Tom if the county put in a new cattle guard or gate, and he said, "No, not a thing, but you know, the horses didn't seem to want to leave anyway."

Mary wrote,

We owned one of her pinto mares. Old "Paint" raised my kids. My husband, Grant, went to her place in about 1950 and bought the filly as a yearling and trailed it home with a neighbor who also bought some of her horses. Paint lived to be twenty-eight years old.

I never met her, but I heard that Fannie was quite a nice person who always had time to help the young women who wanted to become horse people.

Bill Huntington, author of *They Were Good Men and Salty Cusses*, wrote: "Of all the women riders that I ever saw on the hurricane deck of a bucking outlaw horse, I think Fannie Sperry had them all cheated. . . . She rode her bucking horses slick, fair, and honest. . . . There never was any easy horses picked for her. They filled the chute and Fannie rode whatever horse her number called for."

He also described her as "a quiet, dignified lady that everybody liked."

Dee Marvine, author of *The Lady Rode Bucking Horses*, visited Fannie shortly before the cowgirl died at age ninety-five, and she brought a recording of an interview with Fannie at a rodeo from her bronc-riding days. "The tape started with the roar of the crowds, and when she heard that, she sat straight up in her bed and got such a huge smile on her face," Marvine said. "Fifteen years just melted from her."

"I have never tired of rodeo in my life," Fannie wrote. "I hope there's an arena in Heaven . . . that's where you'll find me."

As Heather Raftery wrote in an article for *Range* magazine,

Maybe in her last moments Fannie Sperry Steele again heard the roar of the crowds, the slap of her skirt on the saddle, and the jingle of spurs. Maybe she smelled the dust billowing from pounding hooves, her own sweat mingling with that of the animal beneath her, and the distinctive scent of well-worn leather. Maybe she felt the rise and fall of a bucking horse and the feel of air rushing past, blowing her dark hair back and whipping the tails of her silk scarf about her flushed, smiling face.

Maybe she was, once more, World Champion Lady Bronc Rider.

Jane Burnett Smith wore many hats during her life. "For a woman, what else is there after rodeo?" she wrote in *Hobbled Stirrups*. "Rodeo men who retire from the arena usually settle for breaking and training horses, managing ranches, teaching in one of the newly formed 'rodeo schools,' or even tending bar or gambling. But women? That's a different story."

Jane did not retire to knitting neck scarves in a rocking chair. She quit rodeoing to join the Women's Army Corps in the early 1940s and learned to fly. Following her service, she returned to Montana, married Woody Smith of Gilt Edge in 1946, and they had two children, Camille and Loren. The Smiths owned Bar 87 at Windham, and Jane dealt blackjack near Glacier Park one winter and the next summer moved to Chico Hot Springs to play the organ. After they sold the bar, they moved to Arizona.

During her post-rodeo life, Jane became a certified scuba diver and underwater photographer, sold real estate, and dealt blackjack in Reno. She also worked as a medical transcriptionist and as a substitute creative writing teacher, and she wrote several Spanish-English puzzle

Jane Burnett Smith publicity photo COURTESY OF CAMILLE SMITH

books for the National Textbook Corporation—despite not knowing Spanish.

"My husband said, 'Are you crazy?'" Jane related in an interview, "but I got a (Spanish-English) dictionary, used the simplest verbs, and took it to a translator to go over. There were only a few corrections." The clues were written in English, and the answers would be in Spanish, she explained. These books were still earning royalties and being used in US and overseas high schools when she died.

As a young girl Jane wrote ranch romances and was published in a short-story anthology in 1955. In 2000 she published her first mystery novel with a rodeo background, *If At First . . .*, followed in 2001 by *Always Standing By*, and her memoir, *Hobbled Stirrups*, was published in 2006.

Rodeo riding requires a certain personality, an element of competitiveness and risk taking, Jane said in looking back at her life. "It was a little like pool-playing. I wanted to show what I could do—do what the big boys do."

With rodeo Jane "felt like I belonged for the first time in my life. I worked so hard to be a part of a group. That was as much of a struggle as the riding was."

"I never knew from day to day where it [her riding] would lead," she said. "I always thought I'd become a great bronc rider, but I never did." Jane was proud of what she accomplished, however. "I got by on sheer guts. When I started out I didn't know what I was doing. Nobody told me what to do. I just did it, and learned on my own. I just stayed on as many jumps as I could."

Riding hobbled allowed this cowgirl, who was just five feet, two inches tall and

Jane Burnett Smith gets credit in the movies.

COURTESY OF CAMILLE SMITH

110 pounds, to ride tougher horses, she said. "It was easier to ride saddle broncs than bareback or steers. With steers, it was just pure strength in the arms, and that was harder for women to keep in position. I was not that strong."

She did ride with Bobby Brooks during a three-day rodeo in Forsyth at one point in her career. "Bobby was used to riding big old rank wild horses out on the range, and she was one of the few professional women bronc riders who did not hobble her stirrups."

Jane mostly did exhibition rides, for "mount money." Many times, she said, she was the only woman at the rodeo. "I only rode in competition with other women eight or ten times in my career, even at Madison Square Garden." She rode at the Garden in 1941, the last year women were allowed to compete in bronc riding on the men's circuit.

"Women's riding was waning. Promoters didn't want to mess with us and start to have to have different stock for women," she said.

"My own small role in the history of rodeo may or may not be considered typical of rodeo people in general," Jane wrote in her memoir. "I am kind of a 'has-been who never was' but I damned sure gave it a try. And just because a man or woman never reached the championship level, maybe never even came close, is no reason to write them off as failures. There are lots of things besides riding ability and guts that determine who makes the grade and who does not. It is no disgrace to fail. The only disgrace is in not trying."

As far as a highlight from her life, she told a reporter, "How can you select a highlight from a life that varied from riding broncs in Madison Square Garden to struggling to be accepted in the movie business to eventually joining the army, raising a family, dealing blackjack, and being a published author? Each one of these lives provided its own highlight."

Jane died in Chandler, Arizona, on November 15, 2011, just a month short of her ninety-second birthday. She has been nominated to the Cowgirl Hall of Fame.

———

Bobby Brooks married Corwin "Bud" Kramer on July 24, 1943, while he still served as a cavalryman in the army. After he came home from the war, they began buying land in Garfield County.

"You had an awful hard time getting a few dollars," Bobby said, but she followed her dad's advice: "'Whatever money you get, buy land because it's not going to stay that cheap.'"

In 1945, she related, she made an offer of $3.33 an acre for thirty sections of land, "a ridiculously low offer," but the only one received. "I wrote them a check and didn't have no money," she admitted.

Her dad, the former sheriff, was upset with her. "They'll throw you in jail and you'll never get out!"

"I knew my dad and my husband were mighty unhappy with me, but I did it," she said. With only five hundred dollars in her checking account, she called a land brokerage firm to borrow the rest of the money. "I was young then, and my motto was, always shoot for the sky, you'll fall someplace in between."

In the 1930s, failed homesteaders had left their horses to run wild across the prairie. Mechanization and World War II, with men going off to war, contributed to the glut. By the 1940s, "there were horses on every hill," old-timers recalled. Bobby's adopted son, Gary Crowder, said that early in his mother's life, "they were just starting to fence the country, but you could ride from the Missouri [River] to the Yellowstone and not hardly open a gate."

"It was a land that was overpopulated with horses—running free and inbreeding," Bobby said in an interview later in life. "It was a business opportunity for someone willing to work hard."

Ranchers who took over the land rounded up these wild horses and sold them to the Kramers, who broke them and sold them as riding or draft horses. Bud and Bobby captured as many as ten thousand horses a year and shipped entire trainloads from Ingomar.

A trend from the Southwest created a growing market for the new "short horse," or quarter horse. The Kramers, along with Benny Binion, a Las Vegas casino owner who owned a Montana ranch, were instrumental in bringing in first-rate sires and developing a top-notch quarter horse herd in an area Montanans call "The Big Dry."

That's how Bobby, who was a lifetime member of the American Quarter Horse Association, got her start breeding and training award-winning quarter and cutting horses.

Together Bobby and Bud formed one of the largest horse ranches in the United States, the Kramer Horse Ranch, at Cohagen, under the Hanging Diamond A brand, which grew to more than 150,000 acres.

In 1962 Bobby got her pilot's license. "We just couldn't get around" that large ranch. She flew to check on their horses and occasionally to herd a wayward bunch.

One day she went out to find an older wild mare they had been having a hard time rounding up. She saddled her fastest horse and left him in a corral. Then she climbed into her Cessna 172, flew until she found the mare, and chased the horse with the plane until she ended up near the corral. Bobby landed in a field, mounted her horse, and roped the renegade mare nobody else had been able to catch. "I thought the rope was too short, but I throwed it anyway."

"She could rope anything," her son, Gary, commented.

Bobby said of this wild pinto, "I felt sorry for her, for her lost freedom, and if she'd got out, I'd be happy for her."

Bobby continued to fly around the ranch and later competed in and won air races.

In 1962 the Kramers purchased an eighty-acre ranch near Billings. Bobby's father was ill, and she wanted to be closer to a bigger town. Around that time, when she was close to fifty years old, she went to business college.

Twenty-two-year-old Gary Crowder came from Malta in 1968 to help run the place and became a partner in the Kramer-Crowder Horse Ranch. Bud and Bobby had never had children of their own, but the Kramers became fond of Gary, and they formally adopted him. Gary, his wife, Linda, and son, Kale, still run the quarter horse ranch. Linda teaches barrel racers and trains barrel and cutting horses.

Tragedy struck in 1979, when Bud was killed in a vehicle accident. Bobby related that she was following him, pulling a horse trailer, when she saw the truck veer off the road. She speculated that he may have had a heart attack.

Bobby continued to work hard with her horses on the ranch and was still riding almost to the day she died. In the 1950s she had completed a one-day endurance race on one horse, riding 140 miles from Billings to Miles City. "She made it in nineteen hours, thirteen minutes and fourteen seconds, coming in third," Gary related, "and the next morning she got up and trailed horses."

Not to be outdone by her younger self, in 1989, at the age of seventy-six, she was one of two women among forty-four drovers to ride fifty miles in the Great Montana Centennial Cattle Drive.

Bobby had a houseful of awards for the horses she raised and trained, including AQHA Grand Championships and All-Around Championships, which include six won when she was eighty-one years old. At age ninety she won one of four high-point awards at the Billings Saddle Club, of which she was a charter member from 1939. Bobby was a lifetime member of the American Quarter Horse Association, Montana Quarter Horse Association, and Montana Cutting Horse Association. She was featured in the documentaries *I'll Ride That Horse* and *The Last Stronghold*.

But her highest award, and one she was most proud of, was her induction in the National Cowgirl Hall of Fame in 2000.

Bobby Brooks Kramer died January 5, 2008.

"Montana's women adapted to the frontier life,
significantly influenced the state's history, and
lived lives that were distinct but as important
as the men's lives."
—MONTANA, THE MAGAZINE
OF WESTERN HISTORY

CHAPTER FIFTEEN

The 1950s

"I would definitely do it all over again."
—ANN SECREST HANSON

The cowboy spurred forward and back as the outlaw bronc kicked toward the sky with his hind legs, then pawed the air with his front hooves. Man and beast melded, the cowboy absorbing the blows like he had springs in his body. The eight-second whistle blew, and the cowboy leaned over to grab hold of the pickup man, nearly losing his hold upon learning he'd been picked up by a woman.

Ann Secrest Hanson was born at Fort Peck, Montana, when her dad worked on building the Fort Peck Dam (the third-largest earth-filled dam used for power in the United States) there. Growing up on her grandmother's homestead at Flat Creek, north of Jordan, Ann rode a horse to get to school. "I always loved horses," she said in an interview. "I drew pictures of horses and they were hanging all over the walls at home."

The one person in her immediate family who was "horse crazy," Ann admired her cousins, the Berrys, "a bunch of wild girls," and wanted to pattern herself after them. Their father, Leo Berry, gave Ann her first saddle, and there she felt at home. She said she also loved reading about Fannie Sperry Steele. "She is one of my idols."

Ann Secrest Hanson, pickup man COURTESY OF ANN SECREST HANSON

About the time Ann was ready for high school, her folks sold the ranch and bought a dairy farm near Missoula. "I hated that farm," she said, so after graduation she came back to eastern Montana and worked for the telephone company in Miles City, then began working for a ranch.

That's where she met a young rodeo cowboy, Walt Secrest, who was breaking horses on a neighboring ranch. "I'd ride back and forth between the spreads, and that's how we met."

She married her cowboy, and they bought a twenty-five-section ranch at Cohagen, where they raised cattle, sheep, and registered quarter horses and bucking horses. They had one son, Cotton, who now ranches at Hardin.

Ann worked for the Miles City Auction Company to help buy cattle for the ranch, trained quarter horses for the track to market the colts better, and attended a stockman veterinary school in Fort Collins, Colorado, to learn how to pregnancy test and perform cesarean sections on cows. "I never let anything stop me if it would help the ranch," she said—not even working with men on other ranches who may have looked sideways at a woman doing a man's job. "Some cowboys didn't seem to mind and others totally ignored me. I didn't really care. The best way I found to get along was to always ride a good horse, do a good job, and not say anything. Pretty soon they started noticing and would invite me back to help."

"I did everything I needed to do to run a ranch. For fun, I bull-dogged and rode steers, wrote poetry . . . judged Queen contests and broke my own horses to ride," she wrote in her book *I Did it My Way*.

Since she had ridden most of her life, Ann "fell into the rodeo life with ease." She started out barrel racing. "I won a lot of buckles, but never won a championship saddle," she said, although admitting she won a trophy in barrel racing after she turned fifty and joined the Old Timers Association.

"It was no big deal, but it's a nice little trophy," she said modestly.

Barrel racing was not exciting enough for Ann, so she tried bull-dogging, "but I had too many wrecks. I just wasn't strong enough." She said she also broke a lot of horses and tried bronc riding, "but I wasn't very good at it."

Then she began team roping with her husband, who also worked as a pickup man at the Miles City Bucking Horse Sale. This event has been a nationally known rodeo and sale since 1951, when Bob Askin and Paddy Ryan were the first pickup men and Cy Taillon emceed. Alice Greenough served as secretary of the organization in 1958.

In 1962 one of the pickup men had to go home, leaving a vacancy. As the organizers wondered what to do, Ann's husband suggested that she could help.

"It didn't scare me at all," she wrote. "I had watched enough to know where to be to help the other pickup man."

A pickup man is a skilled horseman and roper who removes riders from bucking horses, rescues them when they become entangled in rigging, and removes the flank strap from horses to get them out of the arena.

"Picking up bucking horses requires many things the average person does not see," Ann wrote in her book. "First, the person has to be in good shape, as you use every muscle in your body. Good, broke, big saddle horses are a must. Having the horses in shape is necessary, as they run and have big stout broncs hanging off them for hours at one performance."

"Ann did a real fine job," wrote T. J. Walter of Watkins, Iowa, director of the PRCA, PRCA board secretary-treasurer, and secretary of the Pro Rodeo Hall of Fame. "Good horsemanship is just part of what it takes to be a good 'pickup' person. It takes good roping skills, nerves of steel, and an ability to respond quickly and intuitively to a predicament in the arena."

One of her jobs was to exercise about twenty head of pickup horses every day for the two months before the Miles City Bucking Horse Sale.

Ann apparently impressed the producers, because they hired her the next year and she rode pickup for the next twenty-five years. This is an unusual occupation for a woman, and she is the only woman she is aware of who has done this on the PRCA level.

"They [the PRCA] would never sell me a card," she said, "but if the rodeo committee would call in and say 'OK, we know her,' they could hire me. They never turned me down."

She said, "I've always regretted not being able to get my professional card. It would've been a nice feather in my hat."

Ann experienced discrimination against women in the men's rodeo world, something that continued even twenty and thirty years after World War II ended. For the first couple of years she worked pickup, she was paid a lower rate than the men. However, Ann negotiated and was paid equally from then on.

But she admitted that she received many compliments on her work from national RCA rodeo announcer Cy Taillon, called "the golden voice of professional rodeo" and "rodeo's Walter Cronkite." That made her feel "worthy," she said.

Ann Secrest Hanson, pickup man COURTESY OF ANN SECREST HANSON

Picking up was "hard work, but it was all terribly exciting and so fulfilling as a rider," Ann said. "Some [inexperienced] riders get so scared you gotta tell them to 'get off.'" Some would grab her around the neck and not let go, nearly pulling her off her horse.

"I've been jabbed and grabbed, and once I had the buttons torn off my shirt, showing my bra," she related. "I had to ride through the arena trying to button my shirt." No, she wasn't embarrassed. "It's just part of the job.

"Most of the cowboys were very polite and said 'Thanks, Ann' as soon as I helped them off."

Ann was injured in Rapid City, South Dakota, by a fellow pickup rider who was inexperienced and riding a horse that wasn't "well-broke." When she hazed the bronc into the pen, the young man couldn't stop his horse and it crowded into the pen "with me and the bronc and bent my foot straight back." It wasn't broken, but she spent the night with her foot elevated so she could ride again the next day. She says she suffers from arthritis in that foot and ankle today.

"I got bucked off my own horse one time," Ann said. It happened when a rider accidently spurred Ann's horse in the flank when she picked him off his bronc. "And I got knocked out a time or two." She said once a bronc came out and hit her horse broadside. She hit her head and the "lights went out."

"You gotta be tough," was her observation.

In all the years as a "pickup man," Ann said only one bronc rider refused to allow her to pick him up. "I ain't gettin' off on you," he yelled when she rode up alongside him.

"Keep ridin' then," she said.

The other pickup man, her husband, rode up and jerked him off his horse and told him, "Don't you ever do that again!" After that Ann just rode behind that particular cowboy and "let him take a beatin'" while he waited for another pickup man.

Ann not only helped run the ranch near Cohagen and raised quarter horses, but she was also constantly on the road, riding the rodeo circuit for twenty-five years. "It can be a tough life," she admitted. "You gotta be young to do it . . . and you have to love it and be willing to sacrifice a lot to go down the road."

The Secrests were neighbors to Bobby Brooks Kramer, but Ann and Bobby did not get along. "We were not friends. She was older and I think she saw me as competition. I don't know why, she was well known as a bronc rider." The two strong-minded, feisty women did get into fisticuffs one day in Miles City "until the sheriff came along and broke it up."

A good friend from the well-known Askin family was Margorie Askin Griebel, sister of Birdie Askin Johnston, both Bob Askin's daughters.

In addition to PRCA rodeos, Ann also helped put on amateur, Indian, college trials, and kids' rodeos and did pickup for those. She

Ann Secrest Hanson COURTESY OF ANN SECREST HANSON

also helped start a rodeo company and put on rodeo schools with champion bronc rider Bill Pauley and bull rider, Wally Badgett, as instructors. Ann was also active in the Northwest Ranch Rodeo Association and edited their monthly publication called the *Piggin String* for many years.

"We finally bought a camper because we had so many young kids coming with us, and I'd cook for them."

After Ann and her husband divorced in 1986, she continued to ride pickup with her son, Cotton, who had started picking up with his parents as a teen. Being able to work with him was one of the highlights of Ann's life. Cotton continues to rodeo as a pickup man and compete in roping events, Ann said, but mostly devotes his time to roping and riding on his own ranch near Hardin.

"Those were great years of performing a feat that few, if any, women have had a chance to do in a lifetime," she wrote. She was honored to have worked with some of the biggest rodeo producers: Reg Kesler, J. J. Smith, and Sonny Linger.

Another highlight of her life was when Jay Harwood, RCA announcer from Chinook, Montana, nominated her for the Cowgirl Hall of Fame in Fort Worth, Texas.

Harwood wrote in his letter to the Hall of Fame:

In the truest sense, she's a cowgirl, an outstanding horsewoman and individual. She was ranch reared and knows what it takes to run a ranch, maintain her love for livestock and rodeos, perpetuate the ideals of a Montana cowgirl.

I had the opportunity to see Ann in action in the arena picking up broncs and saving cowboys at the famous Miles City Bucking Horse Sale for a number of years and other top rodeos in Montana. She earned herself the respect and reputation as one of the best in the business and she can ride and rope as good as any cowboy that I have ever known.

Another pro-rodeo cowboy, Wally Badgett, wrote: "Actually 'Cowgirl Hall of Fame' could be considered pretty tame for Ann . . . 'top hand hall of fame' might be more fitting. In these times when you hear comments like 'She can do it just like a man,' Ann can do it better than most men when it comes to cowboying. . . . I know, because she has picked me off a lot of bucking horses."

Another compliment that thrilled Ann was from announcer Cy Taillon in an interview with the *Denver Post:* "Ann has the ability to do a man's job on horseback in the arena, yet can and does dress and act the feminine lady she is at the party at night."

Shirley Stuver, writer for the *Powder River Examiner* in Broadus, wrote:

Seeing a working queen of rodeo and horsemanship . . . pickup bucked out riders for an eight hour stretch . . . with never a miss and a bit of TLC added, and then assist . . . in immediate area clearing in foot-deep mud, which wore out several pickup horses in one afternoon.

Then presiding at breakfast on Monday morning with all the bruises covered by feminine attire, and taking time to further charm adoring fans as she spoke of the bum calf she brought to the sale to feed, because it couldn't stay on the ranch alone.

The induction in November 2003 "touched me deeply," Ann said. "I think back on the many things I've done that others would have loved to do but didn't have a chance. I happened to be in the right situation where I could do them. There are women who are as good, but they weren't able to exercise their potential. I thank God for all of my successes and for overlooking my failures."

At the induction ceremony Ann was onstage, receiving her awards: a plaque, a medal, and a pair of custom-made Justin Full Quill ostrich boots. Then the emcee told how Ann had watched aspiring young cowboys hone their skills at the Secrest Rodeo schools and youth rodeos, and how she had commented that she had always hoped one of those little cowboys or cowgirls would make it to the National Finals and she could go watch.

Then a young man came bounding up the steps to give her a big hug. It was Montana's Dan Mortensen, six-time world champion saddle bronc rider and world all-around rodeo champion. He had been a student in the Secrests' rodeo school, and Ann had picked him off his first professional saddle bronc.

"It just thrilled me to death," Ann said. "And he gave us tickets to watch him at the [National Rodeo] finals in 2003." Mortensen won his sixth championship that year, tying the record with legendary cowboy Casey Tibbs. Ann was as proud of Mortensen as if he'd been her own son.

Ann is now retired and married to Robert Hanson, a quarter horse breeder, and they live on a ranch along the Little Missouri River in the Badlands of North Dakota. "I just quit riding last year," she said. "I've had both knees and both shoulders replaced from all my wrecks, and then my horse got too old and I had to put him down." Without a horse now, she misses riding but spends much of her time writing cowboy poetry and traveling around to cowboy gatherings, reminiscing about the "old days" of ranching and rodeoing. "I would definitely do it all over again."

Her listing on the Hall of Fame website reads: "Ann Secrest Hanson has lived a life of quiet dedication devoted to every facet of ranching and rodeo."

In a poem titled "The Induction" Ann wrote:

I would not trade my lifestyle, tho very hard and harsh at times, for the satisfaction that it brings
To be honored by one's peers, and all the great women out there, who helped to tame the west
Was to me, the height of my western career, and let me know, that to the world, I had really done my best.

CHAPTER SIXTEEN

Modern-Day Cowgirls

*"He who is not courageous enough to take risks will
accomplish nothing in life."*
—MUHAMMAD ALI

Women riders today can compete on rough stock in amateur rodeos, but if they want to do it professionally, the only option is to enter the men's field at PRCA rodeos. And only two are currently taking on that challenge: thirty-six-year-old saddle bronc rider Kaila Mussell, who's been competing in saddle bronc riding for ten years, and twenty-one-year-old bull rider Maggie Parker, who started winning money at sanctioned rodeos in 2012.

The Women's Professional Rodeo Association (WPRA) is the descendent of the Girls Rodeo Association (GRA) formed in 1948; the name changed in 1981. The WPRA is the oldest women's sports association in the United States, and it is the only one governed entirely by women. In 1990 it won a lawsuit that allows it to remain an all-female association.

While the GRA grew out of cowgirls' desire to compete in rough-stock events, the WPRA's primary sanctioned event is barrel racing, usually in conjunction with PRCA events. Barrel racers compete for millions of dollars each year, and contestants are ranked nationally, based on how much money they earned in competition.

(Today's top racer, Brittany Pozzi of Victoria, Texas, has so far earned $1,665,497 in her career.) The top riders go on to compete in the Ram National Circuit Finals Rodeo in Oklahoma City, Oklahoma, in April, and the top fifteen at the end of the rodeo season are invited to compete at the Wrangler National Finals Rodeo in Las Vegas in December.

The WPRA also has an all women's division, and the rodeos feature breakaway calf roping, tie-down calf roping, team roping, bareback riding, and bull riding, in addition to the barrel race. Contestants count points earned in competition to qualify for the Women's National Finals Rodeo each October at the Cowtown Coliseum in Fort Worth, Texas.

The WPRA has added junior divisions and in 2007 began recognizing a junior world champion barrel racer.

From seventy-four original members in 1948, the organization has grown to more than twenty-five hundred worldwide, including Canadian provinces and Australia, and is headquartered in Colorado Springs, Colorado.

The WPRA's women's division once included bareback and bull riding. However, the organization has backed off women's rough-stock events, handing out its last world titles in bareback and bull riding in 2008.

"We were trying to find balance as an association, and interest had fallen off among our members in rough-stock events," stated WPRA's Ann Bleiker in a 2012 interview. "It didn't make sense to keep doing it." The WPRA now focuses on the more popular roping and barrel racing.

Jan Youren of Idaho, five-time world champion bareback bronc rider who began in the 1950s, faults today's pro-rodeo's minimum age requirement of eighteen for limiting women rough-stock riders. The ruling was initiated by the PRCA and adopted by the WPRA in the mid-1990s.

"That was definitely the downfall," she said in an *American Cowboy* interview. "You have to start things when you're young and invincible. By the time women are eighteen, they're thinking about other things." Youren said she is disappointed that the sport seems to be fading away.

"It made my fifty years amount to nothing," she said.

Jonnie Jonckowski, World Champion Female Bull Rider, retired from competition in 2000 when she was forty-six, and she now runs a nonprofit therapeutic riding organization in Billings. She, like Youren, was deliberate in trying to blaze a trail for women in rough stock: "That's why I campaigned so hard. I'd like to know that what I did all those years ago meant something. I know there are girls out there like me who crave that adrenaline."

She believes women's rough-stock competition received a huge blow when the WPRA discontinued those events: "It lost its organization, and it lost its home." Jonckowski would like to see a women's version of the Professional Bull Riders Association that would stage events at the PRCA rodeos.

The Ranch Rodeo Association is one organization that might help bring women back into the rough-stock arena. The Women's Ranch Rodeo Association and Ranch Cowgirls Rodeo Association feature team competitions in sorting, trailer loading, doctoring, tie-down (mugging), and branding. However, the Working Ranch Cowboy Association's World Championship Rodeo held in Amarillo, Texas, in November listed Ky Gripp of Texas as the 2013 Champion Women's Ranch Bronc Rider.

No Montana women currently compete in rough-stock events.

———

In 1988 eleven-year-old Rachael Myllymaki of Arlee was the second-youngest barrel racer ever to qualify for the Wrangler National Finals Rodeo in Las Vegas (before the rules were changed so women have to be eighteen). Competing for the fifty-thousand-dollar purse at the season-ending championship event for the PRCA, she had already won twenty-seven thousand dollars and had twenty-three victories in her first season of pro rodeo.

"It's extraordinary that an eleven-year-old is this good," Lydia Moore, executive secretary of the WPRA, said in an interview that year. "A barrel-racing rider has to have a lot of courage because you're riding the horse extremely fast and asking him to stop and turn quickly."

Even the defending champ, eighteen-year-old Charmayne James Rodman of California, acknowledged Rachel's prowess before the finals. "If anyone has a chance to break my times, it's her," she said. "She's quite a cowgirl."

"Charmayne was a wonderful mentor," Rachael said in a recent interview. "She has natural grace, is a good hand, and is great with horses."

Rachael came in ninth in the finals that year, but she continued to rack up wins and championships all over the country during her career. She was eight-time Montana Circuit Barrel Racing Champion, National High School All-Around Champion in 1994–1995, and while attending the University of Montana won the Collegiate Rodeo Championship in 1996. Rachael also won championships at the Calgary Stampede, Cheyenne Frontier Days, and the Laughlin River Stampede in Nevada in the late 1990s. In 2009 she ranked twenty-first nationally in WPRA standings and won the California circuit title that year.

Rachael has been at home on the back of a horse since an early age.

When she was adopted into the Myllymaki family at age six, her parents presented her with a pony. "It was scary because he looked so big, and I was afraid I'd fall off and get stomped on," Rachael said in an interview. "But I found out fast was more exciting than slow. It was fun. My heart would start pounding, and I could finally race my mom."

Her mom, Judy, was a barrel racer herself, and she began teaching the youngster. By age eight, Rachael had won the Western Montana Cowgirls Association junior division title. While Rachael was the second youngest to qualify for the National Finals Rodeo (NFR) in 1988, Judy became the oldest, at fifty-four, to qualify in 1998, holding that distinction until 2005.

"I wasn't afraid for her as far as her abilities were," Judy said of the 1988 finals, "I was afraid the roar of the crowd might unsettle her, but she wasn't fazed by it."

The mother-daughter team later produced a video, *Barrel Racing with Judy and Rachael*, showing the techniques and stations of the sport, and they both trained horses and riders on the family ranch in Arlee. Judy runs Myllymaki Barrel Horses with her husband Gene and still barrel races.

"It was a good time in Montana," Rachael recalled. "The community was so supportive and showed me such kindness. If you put in the work, they're behind you."

The thirty-six-year-old is also still racing on the professional circuit. "Every time I go through the gate, I go into it with ice in my veins, trying to win. I practice at home, and then I go in and put my best foot forward. That's all you can do—anyplace in your life."

Rachael gives a lot of credit for her success to her horses. "It's a team effort. You're only as good as the horse you ride." She said she is in the building-block stage right now, training colts. "I want to know my horse from top to bottom, every reaction when I push a button. I have a complete relationship with each one. They're my best friends and my business partners."

She admits, "I'm probably more that way [friends with her horses] than others, but I know them and they know me, and I think they're willing to give that little extra for me. Inches make a difference when there's money on the line."

Lately, she said she is looking for "the perfect indoor/outdoor horse—one that performs as well in indoor arenas as outdoor—that would give me an opportunity to win a world championship." The next best thing would be to own two excellent horses, one for indoor and one for outdoor races.

Rachael has lived in California for the last several years and has invested in land and rental property to make a living. While her grandfather was still alive, she said, she bought cows and ran them on his ranch.

She also gives private lessons to young girls. "I like to lend a help-ing hand to girls who ask," she said. Rachael sees future opportunities for women in rodeo. "I think we're headed for a big change. I think the PRCA and the WPRA will come together."

She doesn't see an increase in women's rough-stock events, how-ever. "There are a few out there, but not a big enough number." Rachael never tried riding bucking stock, "not on purpose," she said with a laugh. Her mother, Judy, did, however, when she was young, riding buffalo for entertainment between events at rodeos where her father was a stock contractor.

Her advice for young cowgirls: "Work hard. Ride like you want it, but act like you don't need it." She said she wishes the age limit hadn't been changed to eighteen, but understands the legality issues. "I feel like a lot of girls could've superseded what I've done. There's a lot of talent and good horses out there. I would love to have seen them make their mark."

"I'm happy to have been there when I was, though," Rachael said.

⌒⌒

"What you get by achieving your goals is not as important as what you become by achieving your goals."

—ZIG ZIGLAR

Theresa Walter of Billings is Montana's current Barrel Racing Cir-cuit Champion, a title she's held for the past three years.

For this barrel racer, as for many, it's a way of life. Theresa grew up on a farm and rode horses when she was little. She started rodeoing in the seventh grade. "I just wanted to do that since the first time I saw it," she said in an interview. "I've always been competitive, always played sports."

Her grandfather bought her a horse at the sale ring. Theresa started working with him immediately, and she was successful from the beginning. "I just love it, from the bottom up," she said. She's trained every horse she's ridden and has even broke some. "I learn every day from the animal."

And Theresa loves competition. "It's not so much the adrenaline as it is you and your animal, the time, effort, and training you've put in and the result of that," she explained. "There's an element of self-satisfaction in it. I like to win. It's a tough, heartbreaking sport. I read once that there are coaches in every sport—except rodeo. We do have friends and family that support us, but it's all about you and the horse.

"Rodeo has become such a specialized sport," she continued. "You have to learn all about the animal, about vet care, and feed and tack. The horse itself is an athlete, such an integral part of what we do." And they are insured as such.

Theresa's current barrel horse, eleven-year-old Licorice, is a dream to compete with. She's trained the horse since it was two. "She is all attitude. She tries hard every time she goes in the arena. She is all heart!"

It is said in the barrel-racing circles that a rider gets only one perfect horse, but Theresa wants to prove the saying wrong and train another champion like Licorice.

Although she has never qualified for the NFR, Theresa has qualified five years for the PRCA's Ram National Circuit Finals in Oklahoma in April, three times as title winner and three times as average winner. (Once she won the year-end title and the average title in the same year.) "That is huge," she said. "It's hard to do." She explained there are twelve WPRA circuits in the United States, and two from each circuit—one overall winner and one who wins a three-run overall average—go to the finals.

Barrel racers qualify by the amount of money they win, not necessarily by their fastest times, since every arena is a different size and the barrel formation length varies.

Theresa has worked since 1993 as executive secretary of the Northern Rodeo Association, an eight-hundred-member regional

Theresa Walter, Montana's current barrel racing champion COURTESY OF THERESA WALTER

organization that puts on thirty rodeos a year between June and August. Unfortunately, she said her job keeps her the busiest during the time she needs to be competing, but she still competes in twenty-five or thirty rodeos a year that qualify her for the circuit.

"I've done well with the limited number of rodeos," she said. Theresa has been in the top fifty in the world for three years.

Despite the success of many Montana women in barrel racing through the years, none have gone on to become national champions.

Theresa would love to qualify for the NFR. "I'd be lying if I said I didn't. But it takes a lot of money for training, travel, and vehicles. And it's entirely up to the individual to finance herself."

Sponsors are rare in the sport—usually only the top national champions are sponsored for money. "Most sponsors, if any, are for trade." Theresa explained that she trades publicity with a local barn for the use of the barn and feed.

Theresa is friends with Rachael Myllymaki and has also gleaned inspiration from Montana cowgirls' rich rodeo history. She said her grandfather was friends with the Greenoughs, and she has participated in rodeos with Deb Greenough, a champion bronc rider of her generation. "Anything about rodeo has always intrigued me," Theresa said. "I just love it."

Greenough Legacy Lives On

A breeze swirled mini dust devils as horses whinnied, calves bawled, and bulls kicked the slats in the pens. Chuck Henson jiggled his twenty-month-old nephew, Quinn, on his hip while the child's dad, Deb Greenough, rode, much as Chuck's own mother, Margie Greenough Henson, did when he was a baby.

The rodeo tradition still continues in the Greenough clan. Granddaughter Nancy Jane Henson Dorenkamp became a champion barrel racer, team roper, and rodeo producer in Arizona, and granddaughter Leigh Ann Henson Billingsley is also a barrel racer and team, calf, and breakaway roper in Arizona and New Mexico. Margie and Alice's nephew Deb Greenough (their brother Bill's son) won the bareback title at the 1993 NFR in Las Vegas and qualified for twelve consecutive NFRs during his career. And now Quinn, a teenager, participates in high school rodeos, qualifying last year for the Nationals.

While Margie Greenough was still alive, the Greenough family held a mini family reunion at the annual Tucson Rodeo in 1996. As Leigh Ann rode toward the arena of the Tucson Rodeo grounds, she left her father, Chuck Henson, a National Cowboy Hall of Fame rodeo clown, at the chutes with Quinn, while her second cousin Deb took his turn bareback riding.

Just outside the arena to greet her after her barrel run was her mother, Nancy, secretary of rodeos with the PRCA, and her older sister, Nancy Jane, who also performed in the barrel races.

Finally, in the stands was Billingsley's grandmother, Margie Greenough Henson.

"It's definitely a family affair," Leigh Ann, who is married to saddle bronc rider Erick Billingsley, told a reporter from the *Tucson Citizen.* "It's always neat because we all get together here. It's always like a little reunion."

Leigh Ann and Nancy Jane, and Leigh Ann's daughters in turn, are definitely keeping the Greenough family rodeo tradition alive. "We totally grew up around it and traveled all over," Leigh Ann said in an interview from her home in Tucson. "I started barrel racing when I was age ten in the Arizona Junior Rodeo Association," winning her first buckle by age twelve and her first saddle by the time she was in college. "We had fun traveling and it was always a good time together as a family. All summer long we would go with our dad to the rodeos. He would pick us up on the last day of school and drive north," she said.

With a trailer loaded down with a mule, a dog, and props and his two daughters in tow, Chuck made the rodeo rounds, entertaining crowds with his act.

"We are like any family," Leigh Ann said. "If you grow up with race cars, you do racing. We grew up with horses, so we do rodeos."

"That's the way we were raised. It was a way of life," Nancy Jane added. "Mom rode the barrels and Dad was the clown." She didn't think it was that unusual until her fourth-grade teacher told her how fortunate she was to travel like that. "You've done more already than most people do in their entire lives," the teacher told her.

"I've come to appreciate it more the older I get," Nancy Jane said.

Forty-six-year-old Leigh Ann is still competing in barrel racing and roping. In 2006 she garnered the All-Around World Women WPRA Championship as well as the Breakaway Roping Championship. In 2007 she won the Women's Breakaway Championship in the Senior Pro Rodeo event, and in 2002 she won the Barrel Racing Championship and All-Around Championship for the New Mexico Association.

Her daughters—fifteen-year-old Kaylee and ten-year-old Rayna—also compete in barrel racing, pole bending, goat tying, and team roping—"any event offered."

Nancy Jane, fifty-two, says she never rodeoed full-time, but she team ropes with Leigh Ann and her daughters. She won Rookie of the Year in the WPRA Turquoise Circuit (Arizona and New Mexico) about twelve years ago and the top heeling award in team roping on the circuit.

She and her husband, Jerry, own the Salt River Rodeo Company and provide stock for rodeos in Arizona, California, and other South-western states (something her great-aunt Alice also did). She works as an accountant during the week, but on weekends she is involved in taking stock to rodeos, and she competes with her sister and nieces about eight times a year.

Alice and Margie were "awesome, classy ladies," Leigh Ann said. "They were always dressed up, whether they were competing or when they were older and going out. Everybody respected them. To me, they were just fun."

Nancy Jane echoed that sentiment. "They were always a class act. They enjoyed visiting and people always flocked around them. We did a lot of things together—our family is very close. They influenced us in their mannerisms and class and showed they could be bronc riders and still be ladies."

Leigh Ann did try riding a saddle bronc once in Sante Fe. "I thought, *My grandma did it, I can too.* I stayed on him five seconds." Leigh Ann used her husband's saddle with stirrups set farther forward for men's competition. "The way men ride is completely different, and you need more strength in your thighs. My grandmother used lower-set stirrups, and I think I could've lasted if I had those. But I thought I'd try it once."

Unbeknownst to her at the time, her daughter Kayla rode a steer with a bronc saddle after a high school rodeo one time. "And she rode farther than all the boys," Nancy Jane said. This is now an event at the high school rodeos, she added.

Leigh Ann attributes the demise of women's rough-stock riding in the WPRA partly to the "economy, which pushed everybody out of traveling," and the few competitors. She said:

> There weren't enough girls to make it worthwhile. They [WPRA] had to put up the money for the stock and then have only one or two show up.
>
> It's a different life now, not like it used to be when we were growing up. There are so many rodeos, it's such a race now. Competitors fly back and forth, compete, and are gone in a few hours. I don't know if I would've enjoyed that as a kid. When my grandmother and great-aunt were doing it, they'd stay for the entire rodeo and go from one to another as a group.

Leigh Ann and Nancy Jane did have the opportunity to stay for entire rodeos, since their dad was the rodeo clown.

"Women's rough stock will come back around," Nancy Jane predicted. She sees the future of women's rodeo "growing by leaps and bounds when you have the right kind of women involved. People still want to see the classy ladies of the old days. That's the way women's rodeo is going to progress."

Almost twenty years ago women's rodeo in Arizona was nearly extinct. At the time, most women's events were held outside of the state. One day Leigh Ann and Nancy Jane got together with several other women and decided to organize their own rodeo in Arizona.

Every year since, the sisters have been coordinators of the Cactus Series Rodeo in Payson and Cave Creek Fiesta Days in Arizona. The all-women events are normally held before another PRCA-sanctioned rodeo and are co-sanctioned by the WPRA. These events include breakaway roping, barrel racing, and sometimes calf roping.

Since the arena is already set to go and a stock contractor selected, Leigh Ann said they only have to organize riders and judges and get sponsors.

Chuck Henson, now eighty-two, has retired from rodeo, but he and Leigh Ann are also carrying on the Greenough sisters' tradition of working on movie sets in Tucson as stock wranglers and drivers for the actors, crew, and camera trucks.

Nancy Jane said her dad and mother, Nancy, eighty, are still active and often come help her and her husband out on the ranch. "They have always made sure anything we did was enjoyable," Nancy Jane said.

CHAPTER SEVENTEEN

Even Cowgirls Get the Bulls

"Success comes to those who are willing to risk more than other people feel is safe."
—JONNIE JONCKOWSKI

The sign on the chute in Pendleton, Oregon, read MEN ONLY. Lynn "Jonnie" Jonckowski walked up to the sign, slapped it, and said, "Take that!" Then she strode to the chute to mount a snorting, kicking Brahma bull. It was 1991 and the first time a woman had ridden rough stock at the Pendleton Roundup since Bonnie McCarroll was killed in 1929.

Sixty-two years. It had been a long road, both for women's competition and for Jonnie.

From Billings, Montana, Jonnie had a "huge competitive spirit" from an early age. She started competitive swimming when she was five and had dreams of becoming a world-class swimmer, but at age nine an ear problem changed that. Then she ran high school track and as a senior was a contender for a state title, but a quirk in the rules disqualified her. "My dream of a state title in anything was gone," she said.

Jonnie continued to train in junior college, competing in the pentathlon, ranking second in the United States and third in the world. The 1967 Olympics were coming up, and she had a chance to qualify.

But at Nationals she fell while running hurdles and ruptured a disk. The injury sidelined her, and she was replaced on the team.

"I would be lying if I didn't say that I felt lost and alone. I once had a goal. I once had a team cheering for me, a support system. . . . Now what?"

While healing from the injury, she got a job working as a zoning inspector. "It was a good job . . . but I still felt empty," Jonnie said. She tried bodybuilding, played competitive softball, and ran triathlons, "but nothing seemed to fill the void I was feeling."

But she would not give up. "I had to be the best in the world at something before I died," she said. "I don't know where the competition comes from, but it just burns a hole in you."

One day she was having coffee with her mother at a Billings restaurant and spotted a poster advertising an all-girl rodeo in Red Lodge. "I looked at my mom and said, 'I should enter that.' And she said, 'Fine, whatever.'"

Jonnie didn't grow up with rodeo, but she'd always loved horses and riding. When she was fourteen and working on a dude ranch, her boss, Don, told her about the Greenough sisters, how tough they were, but how ladylike they were, even sewing their own clothes. They became Jonnie's idols.

Thinking about the rodeo, "I figured if girls could do this, how hard could it be?" she said. "I would show Don I was just as tough as the Greenough gals."

Jonnie went to a cowboy bar and asked some patrons to teach her to ride a bareback bronc. They may have looked at her like she was crazy, but someone took pity on her and shared his knowledge and equipment.

Two weeks later "I went to the rodeo, wearing a hat about eight sizes too big and with borrowed rigging." Jonnie hung on and scored fifty-two. "The horse scored fifty and I scored two," she laughed. "But I felt the pageantry of the cowgirl riding the rough stuff." She wasn't hooked on rodeo yet, however, and went back to softball and triathlon training.

Then the same cowboy who had helped her prepare for the all-girl rodeo called and asked if she'd like to try riding a bull. She'd never seen bull riding—"It wasn't big on TV in the '70s. But I didn't know enough to be afraid. I was pretty tough. How hard could it be?" she said. "I lasted four seconds.

"It was one big dance and a huge adrenaline rush," she continued. Now Jonnie was hooked. She had her eye on the prize again—a silver medal in the form of a world champion belt buckle.

She looked for a bull-riding school. "I don't know how many I called—at least a hundred—before I found one [in Colorado] that would let me in. They were all too scared to take on the liability for a woman."

Jonnie was the only female student among 105 men, but she stuck it out, riding one-handed like they did. (Women were allowed to ride two-handed in WPRA events.) At the end of the course, she was in the top ten "ride-off" for the school buckle.

She drew a bull named Spotted Dog, "a big gangly, longhorn-looking critter. I hated him. He didn't look good." By this time the contest was down to two riders, and Jonnie was one of them. The prize dangled just in front of her. "If I could ride Spotted Dog, I could very well win."

Jonnie mounted, and the bull charged out of the chute, kicking and twisting. Then he tripped, hooked a horn in the ground, and flipped over. As he got up, he kicked Jonnie in the face, right between the eyes, splitting the skin from her hairline through her left eyebrow, over the bridge of her nose and then into her right cheek.

"That was my first major reconstructive surgery," she said. It left her with a crooked smile and, as one reporter put it, "talking out of the side of her mouth like a gangster."

While she recuperated in the hospital, she learned she'd come in second. "I was told they just didn't have the guts to give it to me. They couldn't have a girl win it."

But it was a huge stepping-stone for Jonnie. She began riding rodeos on the weekend—"a weekend warrior. I felt I had the advantage over other girls [in the WPRA] because . . . I knew how to train, I schooled and competed with men so I was used to bulls that bucked much harder. I could now once again see a world-class athlete inside myself.

"I thought I'd win a world championship in a year." She laughed. "I was pretty cocky."

For the next several years, Jonnie pursued that dream. There were no women competitors in Montana, so she entered national WPRA events. Bull riding for Jonnie was an addiction. "There was a time I'd do anything, I'd sell anything, just to ride another bull."

She quit her job so she could ride more, and she was placing first consistently, getting better venues and better stock. But as she began her tenth year of riding, still without a title, the hard life in "crappy arenas and a wreck waiting to happen" began to take its toll.

"It was physically and financially difficult. When I'd win—maybe $120—I'd be able to eat and I would weigh 140, but when I lost, I quickly went down to 130," the five-foot, nine-inch Jonnie said.

"We were mostly vagabonds," she continued. Traveling from rodeo to rodeo, she and fellow riders would get on the CB radio to find someone who had a motel room but perhaps didn't have enough money to pay for it. "They'd say, stop in, take a shower, leave a buck on the bed." Or sometimes they would put bricks under the bed's legs to raise it up and "sleep three under the bed."

And relationships were hard to develop. "My personal life suffered," Jonnie related. "When my boyfriend tried to hug me, I'd wince from the pain." He didn't stick around to see her through.

"My family didn't understand. My friends saw me go from businesswoman to a broken-down bull rider who couldn't buy a cup of coffee. 'You're crazy,' they'd tell me. Rather than argue, I walked away."

Jonnie did wonder why she was doing this to herself. "The struggle was hard. It was embarrassing. But if I quit without finishing, I would never know whether I had what it took. And it is easy to see where you finish when you quit . . . LAST. That wasn't in my vocabulary. I had given up so much, I couldn't walk away."

Unable to afford health club dues, Jonnie improvised her training, running twelve miles a day, skipping rope, and adopting "Rocky-style" techniques: doing chin-ups in the barn and lifting paint cans full of sand for weights. She taped notes to her mirror: "I am a winner and I have done all that I can, and I deserve to win."

As the World Championship Finals approached in 1986, Jonnie had no idea how she was going to get there. She was trying to refinance her house to lower the payments, she'd burned the last of the cedar siding a friend had stripped from his house, she had no coffee for the morning, and her two dogs' ribs were beginning to show.

"I closed my eyes and prayed," she said. "When I looked out, the sun was shining." Jonnie called her dogs and went for a run. "I felt light and strong and my confidence began to rise."

On her way back she stopped by the mailbox, hesitating in dread of the daily stack of bills. But she opened it and took out a window envelope. *Another bill*, she thought, then looked closer. It read, "Paid to the order of . . ." It was an escrow refund for the exact amount needed to pay entry fees, airfare, and meals for the Finals.

"I looked up to the heavens and dropped to my knees, thanked God and began to sob. . . . The long battle with loss of security, home, food, friends, and a feeling that my God had abandoned me was gone."

Two weeks later she was in Guthrie, Oklahoma, hearing the announcer shout, "Jonnie Jonckowski in chute number five, all the way from Billings, Montana! Let's all cheer the cowgirl on!"

"I nodded, and the bull came flying from the chute. He ducked and dove, but I hung right in there, jump for jump."

The buzzer sounded. She had made it!

Just as she was getting off, the bull suddenly changed directions and his hoof hit the back of her leg. "I thought it had been severed from my body, the pain was so gut wrenching."

Jonnie made it out of the arena with help, but she sat there looking at her calf that had swollen so badly it had split her pant leg. After learning she'd placed second and needed only one more qualified ride from the two rounds left to go, she went to the hospital. The doctor

Opening up the Las Vegas NFR, 1988; score 86 COURTESY OF JONNIE JONCKOWSKI

told her blood was flowing into the leg, but not out, and that she was at risk of a clot. He told her she would never ride again and would probably drag her leg for the rest of her life. Jonnie said he actually demonstrated the dragging leg.

It was devastating news. "I thought my dream was getting away again," she said. "The pain was unbearable, but I thought, *I would rather die than not do this now.*" She wrapped the leg, elevated and iced it that night, and fought a high fever and convulsions. The next afternoon, since she was far enough ahead in the point standings, the judges let her simply stand in the chute while they released the bull.

Jonnie would have to make her third ride that evening, however. She talked to the stock contractor to get information on the bull she'd drawn, and he told her he thought it could be ridden with just upper body strength. "He said I was probably the only one who could ride him that way."

After a quick prayer in the ladies' room, Jonnie went out to meet the huge brindle bull named B12. "He had foot-and-a-half horns that stuck straight out to the side." Four people hoisted her up to the chutes and helped her move her dead-weight leg over the top of the bull's back.

"I was sweating, but I felt good," she said. "My heart pounded and my confidence soared at an all-time high."

"You ready, Jonnie?" the chute boss yelled.

She nodded, and the gate flung open. "The bull jumped clean and straight. I was right in the middle of him, and I could hear the crowd erupt into cheers." Jonnie hung on for dear life, and when the six-second buzzer sounded, she was still straddling the bull.

Tears of joy streamed down her face. "My God! I made it! My God, I made it!"

The rodeo clowns helped her off safely, and she sat behind the chutes while the other riders congratulated her.

Jonnie Jonckowski had her championship buckle.

She won again in 1988, but there still were bull-riding chutes where women were not welcome. Cheyenne Frontier Days was one

The gals that rode, 1988. Jonnie campaigned for three years to have this event at Cheyenne Frontier Days happen. PHOTO BY RANDALL A. WAGNER, THE WAGNER PERSPECTIVE, COURTESY JONNIE JONCKOWSKI

of them. Her idol, Alice Greenough, had ridden there in the 1940s, but no woman had been allowed to compete since. Jonnie had been working to change that for several years, and finally, after her second championship in 1988, she got the chance.

She recalled:

It was really tough to convince those Cheyenne boys to let us ride. Their fear was that we were going to get bucked off and scream and cry. Being a woman in rough stock, you don't even have the luxury of getting hurt. If a man gets hurt, there'll be ten guys out there helping him, but if a woman gets hurt she'd better wave to the crowd and hop out of there under her own power. Then collapse in private.

In Cheyenne, two women were scheduled to ride bareback and two women signed up for bull riding. When Jonnie pulled in, "it was miles of press." Women riding rough stock was a novelty act that drew attention. By the time she was ready to get on her first bull, "I was wearing sixteen microphones under my shirt. History was being made. Everyone wanted to know, 'What does she think? What is she saying?'

"I wanted everything the men had. I didn't want to get my head kicked in anymore for eighty bucks."

Jonnie continued to campaign for the next five years, and finally Pendleton gave the nod sixty-two years after Bonnie McCarroll died. Jonnie had overcome so many obstacles herself, and in doing so, succeeded in eliminating barriers for the women who followed her. "It didn't take guts for me to ride bulls. It took guts to buck the people who didn't want me to do it. But it was well worth the battle.

"I know there are girls out there like me who crave that adrenaline. That's why I campaigned so hard," she said.

After this recognition Jonnie began to command better pay and appearance fees for her exhibition rides. From sleeping in horse trailers and under beds and wondering where her next meal was coming from, she was at the point where "I could demand the limo, the 'Taj Mahal,' the royal treatment."

Jonnie liked this new life a lot, and for a time she hung up her spurs to play under the dazzling lights of Hollywood. She was offered a role in *American Gladiators*, participated in the game show *To Tell the*

Truth, and then played Chance, an outlaw on the TV series *Wild West Showdown*.

"It was pretty fun and a bit surreal, wearing a cowboy suit, riding down the street where all the movies were filmed, with my plastic gun drawn," she laughed. "Chance was a cattle rustling, horse stealing son of a gun."

Although Jonnie was a bodybuilder, had toughed it out on the back of dangerous bulls, and described herself as a "country lady jock," she said, "I'm not a 'chewer-spitter,' not hard-core macho. There's a preconceived idea of what a gal who rides bulls should look like. I love wearing dresses and heels. I like being a lady. The Greenough sisters did the same kind of thing, with femininity."

Jonnie enjoyed her days hanging out with movie stars in Los Angeles, feeling like she owned the world. She got to meet her hero, Alice Greenough ("I was so in awe of them."); Dan Haggerty of *Grizzly Adams* ("still a great friend"); the Nitty Gritty Dirt Band, who wrote a song for her, "The Bullrider Is a Lady"; and singer Neil Diamond.

"I found out he was actually a fan of mine," she said. He called her when he came to Billings, and she met him at Harley-Davidson. Uncharacteristically, Jonnie was tongue-tied. "I stammered, 'Pleased to meet you, Mr. Diamond' and then cringed." Jonnie was a bull rider from Montana, and he was a mega-hit star, "but we just clicked."

She lived with him for a while, which became tabloid fodder. "He's a great guy, a really sweet man," she said, "but that lifestyle just didn't work for me. The 'star thing'—I was past that."

When filming was over, Jonnie learned her mother's cancer was terminal and went home to spend time with her family. "It was an unbelievable emotional drain," she recalled.

Jonnie then went to work as a personal trainer and physical therapist assistant. "From the glitzy life, I went home to my simple A-frame and four acres," she said.

While working at a nursing home, she made the acquaintance of a ninety-nine-year-old woman. "Ruby had osteoarthritis. She was bed-ridden, in terrible pain, and struggled. All she wanted for her birthday

Jonnie and Elvira. The best way to train a donkey to go into nursing homes and assisted living is to let them get comfortable and hang out in Jonnie's living room. COURTESY OF JONNIE JONCKOWSKI

was an Indian pony." Jonnie had a black-and-white paint, so she enlisted the help of staff to move furniture around and brought Buddy right into Ruby's room. "I handed her a grain bucket and said 'Happy Birthday' and right on cue, Buddy whinnied."

Despite being fired for that incident, Jonnie realized she had brought joy to her patient, and that gave her a sense of satisfaction. She thought about how easy it had been to make someone happy. She began to train her own dogs as therapy animals, and in 1998 she started Angel Horses to reach out to the elderly and disabled. Jonnie and other volunteers use rescued animals such as horses, donkeys, dogs, and cats. "My dream is to have sixty acres and a cowboy town," she said.

Through Angel Horses Jonnie is giving the gift of a second chance to both the animals and members of the community. She hasn't been able to accomplish that "cowboy town" dream yet, but she and her

Last wish granted—riding a horse one more time—Dave Jonckowski, Gladys MacLaron, Jonnie J., and Dick Cottrill COURTESY OF JONNIE JONCKOWSKI

volunteers serve as many as one hundred clients a month and turn away that many because of lack of land and an indoor facility. Jonnie has enlisted help from the White Aspen Ranch, a beautiful indoor facility a mile from her place. That helps with the overflow clients and during the winter "so we don't have to turn anyone away." Jonnie, who takes no salary, holds an annual fund-raiser to help defray the costs of the facility.

"We focus on kids that have lost their parents, struggle to fit in at school, or are just lonely and lack confidence. The horses seem to be such healers," she said. About 75 percent of her clients are seniors—"shut-ins, in hospice, last wish, last ride, lonely, what-have-you. All find comfort here with our volunteers and critters, and it hurts deeply to turn down anyone that just is in need of a hug and human and critter touch."

Jonnie says her health is good now, just "gimpy from all the years of abuse. I no longer run but take long walks and spend hours in the gym. I am also an in-home fitness trainer and just love it. I have been a personal trainer for over twenty-five years, and it is great now to go into people's homes and motivate them there."

All the years Jonnie was so focused on her career and goals, marriage and family were never in the picture—except once. In the mid-1980s she found love with "Big T"—Terry Robinson from the Montana Band (formerly the Mission Mountain Wood Band). But a week before they were to be married, Jonnie watched the news on TV: A terrible plane crash had killed all five members of the band, the pilot, and four other passengers. She was devastated.

For the next twenty-five years, love eluded her.

"I did finally find the man of my dreams," Jonnie said in a recent interview. "Six-foot-two, fit, wavy white hair with steel blue eyes, an outdoorsman, secure, and who had a dog bed in every room of his home. A terrific cook and he loved to spoil me. He was diagnosed with stage four cancer, and after a two-year battle I lost him. He did ride my horse once, but we never got that chance to ride off into the sunset . . . but my heart did."

Jonnie was inducted into the Cowgirl Hall of Fame in 1991.

"What I learned about success in my quest for gold is that success comes to those who are willing to risk more than other people feel is safe," she said. "Whatever happens now is a bonus. Just being here, I'm a winner."

Although not a Montanan, another modern cowgirl deserves a word of recognition for her success in rough-stock riding. Jan Youren of Boise, Idaho, started competing at age eleven at an all-girls rodeo her father produced. That first bareback bronc, "in my father's version, threw me so high in the air the birds built a nest in my pocket before I hit the ground. Dad hoped that would take it out of me, but it didn't."

Youren continued to compete for more than fifty years, until the age of sixty-three, when she retired with five world championships in bareback bronc riding, thirteen reserve championships in bareback, and fifteen reserve championships in bull riding. "I said when my granddaughters beat me, I'll quit," she said. One of her granddaughters had won second at the WPRA World Finals Rodeo that year. Youren came in third.

She was inducted into the Cowgirl Hall of Fame in 1993.

CHAPTER EIGHTEEN

Woman Breaks PRCA Barrier

"Winning doesn't always mean being first. Winning means you're doing better than you've ever done before."

—BONNIE BLAIR

October 1941 was the last time women were allowed to compete on the "men's circuit," when Vivian White of Oklahoma won the world champion title for women's saddle bronc riding at Madison Square Garden, New York.

No woman had qualified to ride against men in PRCA (formerly RAA) rodeos since then—until Kaila Mussell came on the scene in bronc riding in 2001 and Maggie Parker in bull riding in 2012.

These women's successes put them in an elite class of women who have broken the gender barrier in professional sports traditionally dominated by men. They have been called "the Danica Patrick of rodeo." Patrick made her mark in the world of professional auto racing, becoming the first woman to win an IndyCar Series race, and by winning the pole position (a leadership position) at the Daytona 500 in 2013.

Danica Patrick summed it up well for all women seeking to follow their own dreams: "You can only lead by example, and I don't necessarily want my example to step outside the box and be a girl in a guy's world," she told an Associated Press reporter as she prepared to take her position in the top starting spot in a race at NASCAR's elite Sprint Cup Series at Daytona in February 2013. "But if you have a talent for something, do not be afraid to follow through with it and do not feel different. Do not feel like you are less qualified or less competent to be able to do the job because you are different. Ignore that and let it be about what your potential is."

———

Kaila Mussell of Chilliwack, British Columbia, entered her first saddle-bronc event in 2001 in Prineville, Oregon. She placed fourth, becoming the first female competitor ever to finish in the money in a PRCA rough-stock event. The next year she came within $150 of filling her professional card by earning a minimum of $1,000 on the pro circuit, and then in 2003 she succeeded. Again, the first woman to do so.

Kaila is still the only PRCA woman saddle bronc rider in North America.

It's not surprising that Kaila ended up in rodeo. It was in the family genes. She grew up on a farm, riding horses and working cattle. Her mom was a rodeo queen, her dad, Jack, was a bronc and bull rider, and her older brother, CEJ, rode saddle broncs and steer wrestled. Kaila was eleven when she started riding steers and barrel racing. Her younger sister, Filene, also became a barrel racer and steer rider.

Kaila also took up trick riding and performed throughout western Canada and at the Calgary Stampede from 1996 to 1999.

An admitted adrenaline junkie, she grew tired of barrel racing and was looking for a new, more exciting challenge. Kaila said she was too old to ride steers (the smaller animals now used for kids' competition), and she wanted to stay in rough-stock riding. At first she thought she'd graduate to riding bulls, but her parents were adamantly against that. "Too dangerous," they said.

"Okay," Kaila said, "so what else can I do?" She broached the idea of riding broncs, and her parents were on board with that. "They've been good about it, very supportive."

Kaila Mussell, the only woman bronc rider qualifying to compete with men in the PRCA since 1941. COURTESY OF FILENE MUSSELL

Kaila was inspired by the cowgirls from the early 1900s and was drawn to rough-stock riding. "I didn't know of any women that currently rode, especially in the modern style of saddle-bronc riding." She decided to go ahead and compete with men, because the WPRA didn't offer saddle bronc competitions. (The organization discontinued its women's bareback and bull riding after 2008.)

It hasn't been easy being the first woman in a male-dominated sport, but Kaila refused to back down when people told her women don't belong in rough-stock events. "I did the research, read the

Kaila Mussell epitomizes the "modern" cowgirl. COURTESY OF JENNA HAUCK

[PRCA] rule book, and found there was no rule prohibiting women, so I went ahead and did it."

"She had quite a lot of ups and downs with people accepting a lady in bronc riding," her father, Jack, told the *Chilliwack Times*. "It took quite a while to win the judges and people over."

Kaila considers her dad her mentor. "We were always raised that if you can do the job, if you're capable, you can do it."

For a while, the negative reactions bothered the perfectionist cowgirl, but now "I am true to myself, and I don't care what others think anymore. I'm just a bronc rider, I don't ask for favors. If I'm capable, then I should be there."

She told an interviewer on U Spur Radio: "I think a lot of the men were sort of scared of me. But I can't help them with their thoughts. If they have a problem because I beat them, I have better things to worry about in life. I'm competing more against the animals than the other riders."

Kaila says she teases and jokes with the cowboys. "I'm not a male-basher—the guys have been really good to me. It's all about having fun, enjoying the ride. For years, I kept hearing 'just have fun,' and finally, I am."

A writer from the *Calgary Sun* asked a saddle bronc rider at the Roughstock Rumble about his female competition. He replied, "Oh yeah, no big deal."

And that's the way Kaila likes it.

"I would say I've been accepted really well," she said. "I don't like to point attention to the fact that I'm the only female in this event. Obviously, I can't help that I am. It's really cool, but I want to be respectful of moving into what's considered male territory."

"Once you know her, you know the battle isn't with anyone but herself," her father said.

Kaila did consider quitting along the way, after several shoulder injuries and broken bones, tired of fighting stirrups and saddles that didn't fit her five-foot, two-inch frame and the immense pressure she put on herself to bring home money every time.

But she found inspiration in a song, "Saddle Bronc Girl," that Canadian country music singer Ian Tyson wrote about her: "Hey, Kaila, what ya gotta do, how far ya gotta go to make a dream come true. . . ."

The song was just the encouragement she needed during this low time in her life. "It helped me put everything in perspective—more toward having fun and enjoying the riding like I used to."

The focus has shifted from the first reaction of "Oh, my gosh, it's a girl" to "Oh, yes, this girl can ride!" As she gained respect for her skills, her thinking became more positive. Kaila is a big believer in a positive mental attitude, and she posts almost daily on Facebook quotes such as:

Fear interferes with success. Success really is not success. Success is a process. To forget the journey is to lose focus of living. Believing in

*oneself, in your own strength, is confidence. Forgetting is disheart-
ening, depressing, darkness.*

Kaila, who sports a multicolored Mohawk, tattoos, and piercings, realizes she has broken new ground on the circuit. "It recently hit me that I am a role model for all people, proving that anything is possible if you set your mind to something and have the drive to carry it through. I'm not a gimmick. I'm a competitor, and I will be around for a long time."

Why does she compete in this rough, dangerous sport? Her answer: "Challenge, adrenaline rush, danger, love of the sport—the feeling of being in sync with a bucking horse." Kaila describes the feeling of being on the back of a thrashing, sunfishing bronc that only wants to shed its unwelcome burden as "thrilling, powerful, connected, reactive, instinctive." And danger is "anything that will get your heart racing and seems scary."

Kaila has had her challenges as well as her successes. As a self-described perfectionist, she is disappointed in herself when she doesn't ride up to her expectations. Being broke, drawing poor buckers, and being injured also get her down. But when she's overcome her obstacles and made a successful ride, she feels "happy, excited, successful, energetic, positive, confident, empowered."

When asked if bronc riding was a career, she said no. "It definitely doesn't pay my bills. I'd call it a passion, an expensive hobby."

What keeps her going is the support she receives from family, friends, and fans, and the fact that she's invested a lot of time and energy in her sport and loves what she does. "Looking at the bigger picture, my goals, why I do what I do."

Kaila still has her dreams: "I would like to qualify for the CFR [Canadian Finals Rodeo], and I would love to be the first woman to qualify for the NFR [National Finals Rodeo], although I don't know if it's within reason now because I'm looking at the financial side of it.

"I don't really plan far in advance—I could die tomorrow—but eventually it will come the time when I feel 'I'm done with this.' It could be two years or ten. But it'll be when I'm satisfied inside."

Kaila Mussell, a roughstock rider, yet a lady in the tradition of her forbears. COURTESY OF
FILENE MUSSELL

And if she wasn't a bronc-riding cowgirl, she says she would probably be a professional snowboarder or surfer or downhill bike racer or motocross—"anything to keep up with the adrenaline rush."

Kaila hopes she will have left her mark on the rodeo world and paved the way for other women.

"I may not be the best saddle-bronc rider in the PRCA, and I may not always make winning rides . . . but I am always out there trying, and showing the world that there are unlimited possibilities for women."

Her advice to girls is "to be there because you love the sport and are serious about it. You have to realize what you're undertaking. No one should just jump in and say, 'I want to do that because it's cool.'

"Always be true to yourself. Only you know what you want and what works for you. This is your life, make the most of it!" Kaila adds. "I will not tiptoe through life only to arrive safely at death."

Jonnie Jonckowski has met Kaila and says of her: "What a hand she is! I just wish women had their own venue that could really show off their talents. I still don't like women competing with the men, but in this day and age, where else do they go?"

Kaila decided to concentrate her efforts in the semi-pro rodeos and ended the 2013 season second in the British Columbia Rodeo Association (BCRA) and Pro-West Rodeo Association and also came in second at the Ranch Bronc Riding Rodeo in Chelan, Washington.

"Yes, I had been hoping to finish the season off first, but I gave it my best," she said. "It doesn't always go the way a person hopes, but I got pretty close. Apparently second is the theme for me right now. Overall, the season was great and I had a lot of fun. I even had the most wins for a season of my career! Obviously, coming from my perfectionist mentality, I could always do better, but when I look back in perspective, things really were pretty good."

———

Since Kaila Mussell opened the gate for women in the PRCA, another young woman, twenty-one-year-old Maggie Parker, has been working to fill her professional card as a bull rider.

Riders over age eighteen who want to apply for membership in the PRCA must first obtain a permit card and then earn at least one thousand dollars at PRCA-sanctioned rodeos during a year. If the permit holder is unable to win the required amount, he or she must repurchase a permit the following year and start over again.

In June 2012 Maggie became the first female bull rider in PRCA history to win prize money. She rode eight seconds, came in sixth, and won $430.

Maggie got her start in a small town of four hundred in Michigan, when a family friend who once rode bulls took her to a rodeo. "I chose bull riding because it looked like fun," she said. "The adrenaline rush is addicting, and the lifestyle is fun."

She started riding at age sixteen, driving two hours to the nearest corral to practice. At seventeen she moved away from home to work in stockyards and on ranches in Oklahoma and Texas to pay for training.

Maggie trains with top bull-riding mentor Gary Leffew in California, who has coached twelve world champions. "She wasn't very good when she came to me, but she had grit. That's what I admire about her. She ain't got no quit in her—she's determined and she works long and hard on it." Her percentage of staying on is 35 to 40 percent, which Leffew says is a normal average for professional riders.

Despite her successes as a woman in a male sport, she still faces an uphill battle in being accepted, especially when she gets bucked off. "What the hell is a woman doing in bull riding?" the men ask incredulously. "This is why girls shouldn't ride bulls; girls aren't made for this."

"They think I do it for a lot of the wrong reasons," Maggie said. "Most people don't like me before they meet me just because they think I do it for attention and for guys and to be in the spotlight and that I don't really care about it."

Maggie is undaunted. "I'm friends with a lot of the guys, but I still hear criticism and comments every day. It's not as bad as when I first started riding. I just keep a good positive attitude and keep pushing toward my dreams."

All riders face what is called "the most dangerous eight seconds" in sports. But Maggie—who is five feet, five inches tall and 130 pounds—is determined not to be bested by her one-ton opponent. She said:

> Bull riding is one of the most dangerous sports because you're up against an animal and you don't know what he is going to do or what he's thinking. You really have to respect them. You can't ride against them, you have to ride with them.
>
> Sometimes it's been harder for me because when you're learning how to ride a bull you're going to get bucked off—and you're going to get hurt. It's just not going to look very pretty while you're riding. It all depends on the person. You're either a good bull rider or you're not. It takes a long time to gain people's respect and get treated the same as the men.
>
> Everybody gets nervous. When you see your bull coming down the chute, your heart starts pumping hard and you get that adrenaline. That's what makes bull riders different from everyone else . . . we have that heart to overcome that fear and to get on anyways.
>
> City folks think it's crazy, but it's just a way different lifestyle than they're used to. I think sitting in an office all day is crazy. I'd much rather work eight seconds and get to travel the country and have freedom and meet people than [work] eight hours in the same office.

Maggie's goal is to get her PRCA card. "Long term, my goal is to make the National Finals Rodeo in Las Vegas."

Rodeo for women has come full circle.

CHAPTER NINETEEN

Injuries

*"Pain is not too great a price to pay for the freedom
of the saddle and a horse between the legs."*
—FANNIE SPERRY STEELE

As the country song says, "Cowgirls don't cry." Even when they're bucked off a nearly half-ton of angry muscle and bone—a wild steer, a bull, or a bronc. These intrepid cowgirls rode with injuries—taped ribs, casts, bruises—just like their male counterparts.

- Ruth Roach, winner of the 1919 Women's Saddle Bronc contest at the Cheyenne Frontier Days, had her left leg crushed at Madison Square Garden in 1933. A year later she was again thrown from her horse and broke her wrist.

- Alice Greenough crushed her ankle at El Paso and was on crutches for two years. At Madrid, Spain, she was thrown and was in a coma for four days. Later in Australia she received injuries to both knees when a horse fell on her.

- Bonnie McCarroll, winner of the 1922 Frontier Days Ladies' Saddle Bronc contest, was killed at Pendleton in 1929 while riding "hobbled." When thrown, she became caught up in her gear and was dragged to death.

- Fox Hastings of Texas, who began rodeoing in about 1916, was once thrown from her horse, and then it fell on her—twice. Her neck appeared to witnesses so twisted they feared it was broken. She was carried from the arena. But about fifteen minutes later, she rode back to the judges' stand in an open car and asked for a re-ride. She got it, rode to the end, and dismounted on her own. Only when out of sight of the crowd did she collapse.

- Tad Lucas was one of the most famous trick riders. At the 1933 Chicago World's Fair, when going under her horse's belly, Tad slipped. She hung there, her horse kicking her with every step as he kept galloping around the arena. Finally she was able to roll free, ending up with a badly broken arm. At first the doctors wanted to amputate. She said, "Absolutely not." They told her she'd never ride again. Within a year she proved them wrong, riding with her arm in a cast.

- Marie Gibson went to London with Tex Austin's troupe in 1924. The first week out, she dislocated her knee, had it wrapped, and came back later for trick riding. But when she stepped off the horse, she felt it go again. The doctor reset it and told Marie to lay off. She did—for two days—then rode again. Marie had to have help saddling and mounting and had to be carried from the stadium, but she kept coming back.

Jonnie Jonckowski says, "I'm pieces and parts. I have scars in more places than most people have skin. It's pretty bad when you know your anesthesiologist by his first name." In addition to the reconstructive surgery on her face after her student bull ride, the leg-threatening injury at her first championship win, and a spiral fracture in her right arm, her worst injury happened on a pleasure ride one evening. Her horse suddenly reared up, bashing Jonnie's brow bone. As she fell to the ground, the horse crashed down on her, snapping ribs and bones. Jonnie lay in the field praying for her life.

"I knew this was the wreck that kills people," she said. But she recovered, wondering "what God has here for me to do. It must be huge."

Then in 2000, doctors discovered a fast-moving tumor in her brain. "I was about two weeks from being blind and six months from being dead." Jonnie underwent surgery and "lost the left jaw, upper jaw, all of my teeth, my palette, the rim of my eye and my cheekbone." Many procedures later, using bone from her hip to rebuild her face, people can't tell the trauma she's had.

"I've been very blessed my whole life. When things would get tough my mom would say, 'Honey, have a little faith.'" The community poured out support for her. "I would not have survived without their love." And she has learned what God wants her to do, with her Angel Horses program.

Kaila Mussell has broken her right wrist, her left collarbone once, and the right collarbone twice. She separated her right shoulder and had surgery, dislocated the left shoulder twice and had two surgeries on it, and has had ACL surgeries on both knees. In April 2014, Kaila was recovering from reconstructive surgery on two broken vertebrae in her neck, but she wrote to her Facebook friends, "I'm optimistic, but I'm taking the injury seriously. I would imagine I'll be back riding broncs again no later than the end of June or early July."

Fitness is key to recovering from and preventing more injuries, she said. An avid fitness enthusiast, she is a certified personal trainer and has her own fitness advice website, kaifit.com. And she is always thinking positive: "If you think, 'What if I do something and hurt that shoulder again?' you probably will. You have to be smarter about how you do things, listen to your body more. Stay active, do strength training (she's a big proponent of core training), and eat right."

Maggie Parker experienced a setback in her career during a rodeo in Cody, Wyoming, in August 2013, when she was thrown off and broke her spine—for the second time—even though she was wearing a protective vest and helmet.

"I was making a good bull ride and I just lost my rope, and he threw me up in the air pretty high, and I landed on the back of my neck, and my body crumpled," she said.

At St. Vincent Health Care in Billings, Dr. Richard Teff, a former military surgeon who served in Iraq, put a rod and multiple screws in Maggie's spine. With that hardware and an external brace, Teff said the broken vertebrae in Maggie's back would heal in about six months, and that she could be back competing in the arena six months after that.

"Now all we have to do is get her to comply," he said.

Maggie told KULR-TV in Billings she had no intention of giving up bull riding. "I don't do it because I want to prove anything. I just do it because it's what I love to do." Maggie said she's looking forward to getting back. "I couldn't change my lifestyle now even if I wanted to really. It's just what I do, and it's what I love to do. It's the best life. You get to travel, meet people, and you're all one big family."

"She's tough, like me. She'll recover," said Jonnie Jonckowski, who visited Maggie in the hospital. "She's got the same spunk I do. She's gonna get up and twist 'em again. I'm certain of that."

Maggie's mother, Susan Parker, said she can't discourage her daughter from getting back in the arena and competing again.

"I think it's really important to let Maggie live her dreams," Susan told the *Billings Gazette*. "I'm not going to stop her. I was a free spirit that hiked all over Africa and Europe when I was younger, got myself in some rough situations, and I know what Maggie's going through. I know that there are a lot of dangers, but I also know that there are a whole lot more rewards."

"It's truly a tough row to hoe for any gal," Jonnie added. "Maggie has a year to think about her bull riding career, and with these injuries, I feel it may be tough for her to come back mentally as well as physically. She is a small gal . . . but she has heart and that is the key ingredient to any sport."

Although barrel racing appears to be less dangerous in terms of injuries, it's not without incident. Theresa Walter broke several fingers and had to have surgery early in 2010. The doctors told her she wouldn't be able to compete until midsummer, but she was back on the circuit as soon as she could be and won her first circuit championship.

Cowgirl Hall of Fame

The National Cowgirl Hall of Fame in Fort Worth, Texas, honors and documents the lives of women who have distinguished themselves while exemplifying the pioneer spirit of the American West. Thus far it has honored more than two hundred women.

Inductees from Montana include Evelyn Cameron (photographer, 2001), Marie Gibson (world champion bronc rider, 2011), Alice and Margie Greenough (world champion bronc riders, 1975 and 1978), Ann Secrest Hanson (pickup man, 2003), Jonnie Jonckowski (world champion bull rider, 1991), Shela Kirkpatrick (custom hat maker, 1992), Bobby Brooks Kramer (bronc rider and quarter horse breeder, 2000), Pamela Harr Rattey (sculptor), and Fannie Sperry Steele (world champion lady bronc rider, 1978).

AFTERWORD

I grew up on a ranch in eastern Montana, riding with my grandmother, Olive May "Tootsie" Bailey Gasser. I knew she was an avid horse-woman who preferred the back of a horse to a dust mop any day. I was twelve when she died, and my dad told me she had ridden the big wild bucking steers in rodeos when she was in her teens.

I have the following newspaper clipping from the *Sunburst Sun* advertising rodeo festivities for August 28, 1922:

Program

> *1:00—Parade of cowboys and cowgirls, headed by Cut Bank brass band.*
> *1:30—Roping and bronc busting.*
> *2:30—Tootsie Bailey will enter competition with entire field, riding wild steers with only one hand on surcingle.*

Tootsie Bailey Gasser, the author's grandmother
AUTHOR'S COLLECTION

8:30—Roundup dance at Sunburst hall. Hammond's famous Glacier Park orchestra. Dance continues until it stops.

And a later recap of the rodeo relates that Tootsie Bailey had won over Marie Gibson in the steer-riding competition.

My grandmother did not continue competing and did not achieve the kind of fame that the cowgirls in this book did. But she gave me that spark of history that led me to write a novel series based on her, and to become well acquainted with the women who conquered the West (even before they could vote) through the golden age of rodeo.

They were the first professional women athletes, who turned their prairie survival skills into a career and held their own against the cowboys.

Bibliography

1976 Hill County, Montana, Bicentennial Committee. *Grit, Guts and Gusto.*

Arctic Circle Productions: arcticproductions.com/From_Cheyenne_to_Pendleton/The_Origins_of_Barrel_Racing.html.

Arizona Daily Star, September 16, 1994.

Arizona Republic, August 23, 1995.

Baumler, Ellen. "The Ladies Busted Broncs," *Distinctly Montana,* Summer 2007.

Bechman, Alexis. "Family Traces Rodeo History Back to the 1920s," *Payson Roundup,* August 24, 2010.

Bragg, Addison. "Her Trick Is Riding," *Billings Gazette,* June 25, 1972.

Brown, J. P. S., "Rodeo Royalty," *American Cowboy,* May/June 2003.

Bryant, Tom. "Trixi McCormick: A Montana Cowgirl," *Western Horseman,* January 1990.

Carbon County News, January 8, 1937.

Clark, Butch, and Helen Clark. "One of the Greats: Trixie McCormick," *Hoofs & Horns,* March–April, 1972.

Clark, Helen McDonald. "She Rode 'em Straight Up."

Clark, Helen. "Trixie Brought Glamour to Rodeo," *Great Falls Tribune,* January 17, 1971.

Disend, Michael. "The Ballad of Jonnie and Big T," *Special Report on Sports,* May–July 1990.

Flood, Elizabeth Clair. *Cowgirls: Women of the Wild West,* January 3, 2000.

Greenough, Alice. "Cowgirls of Yesterday," *Persimmon Hill.*

Gregg, Eddie. "The Heart to Overcome: Professional bull rider recovering from broken back at St. Vincent Healthcare," *Billings Gazette,* August 25, 2013.

Heath, Bryan. "Rodeo 'ropes' family in," *Tucson Citizen,* February 22, 1996.

Helena Independent Record, October 3, 4, 5, 1904.

Hirschfeld, Cindy. "Ride Like a Girl," *American Cowboy* blog, americancowboy.com/culture/ride-girl, November 2012.

"Horsetalk": horsetalk.co.nz/features/sidesaddle-159.shtml "Sidesaddles and suffragettes—the fight to ride and vote" by CuChullaine O'Reilly FRGS, of the Long Riders' Guild Academic Foundation, lrgaf.org.

Interviews with Linda Brander, Leigh Anne Billingsley, Gary Crowder, Jonnie Jonckowski, Kaila Mussell, Ann Secrest, Jane Burnett Smith, Theresa Walter.

Jacobs, Charity. U Spur Radio interview, June 21, 2011.

Jonckowski, Jonnie. "I Just Couldn't Quit," *Living Positive,* premiere issue, 1998.

Jordan, Teresa. "Alice Greenough," 1982.

———. *Cowgirls: Women of the American West,* April 1, 1992.

Kalland, B. "Girls Rodeo Association," *Florence* (Alabama) *Times Daily,* May 10, 1956.

Koerber, Julie. "Jonnie Jonckowski: On the Ride of Her Life," *Yellowstone Valley Woman,* November–December 2006.

Larson, Helen Kay Brander. *Brander Sisters: Let 'er Buck.*

LeCompte, Mary Lou. *Cowgirls of the Rodeo: Pioneer Professional Athletes (Sport and Society).*

Mally, Barbara Greenough. "Alice Greenough, Founder of the Carbon County Museum," *Red Lodge Weekly,* July 21, 1983.

Marvine, Dee. *The Lady Rode Bucking Horses.*

McKelvey Puhek, Lenore. "Fanny Sperry Made the Ride of Her Life," Historynet.com.

Merriam, Ginny. "Celebrating Trixi," *The Missoulian,* May 13, 2001.

Moulton, Candy. "Author of Hobbled Stirrups Dies," *Roundup,* April 2012.

Moulton, Candy. "Hired Out for a Tough Hand," True West, June 2006.

Raftery, Heather. "The Bronc Busters Wore Lipstick," *Range,* www
    .rangemagazine.com/features/winter-10/wi10-bronc_busters.pdf.
Red Lodge Weekly, July 21, 1983.
Roach, Joyce Gibson. *The Cowgirls.*
Rosseland, Wanda (ed.). *The Montana Cowboy: An Anthology of
    Western Life.*
Savage, Candace. *Cowgirls.*
Smith, Catherine, and Cynthia Greig. *Women in Pants: Manly
    Maidens, Cowgirls and Other Renegades.*
Smith, Jane Burnett. *Hobbled Stirrups.*
Stephens, Melanie. "Even Cowgirls Get the Bulls," *Women's Sports
    and Fitness,* May/June 1992.
Stiffler, Liz, and Tona Blake. "Fannie Sperry Steele, Montana's
    Champion Bronc Rider," *Montana, the Magazine of Western
    History,* Spring 1982.
Synness, Curt. "Fannie Sperry Steele," *Helena Independent Record,*
    Curt's Replays.
Wilson, Gary A. "Cowgirl's rodeo riding career began in Havre,"
    Havre Daily News, November 5, 1982.
Wright, P. J. "Avon cowgirls a legend in rodeo history," *Silver State
    Post,* February 1, 2012.
Wyoming Tales and Trails, wyomingtalesandtrails.com

INDEX

About the Author

Heidi M. Thomas grew up on a working ranch in eastern Montana. She had parents who taught her a love of books and a grandmother who rode bucking stock in rodeos. Describing herself as "born with ink in her veins," Heidi followed her dream of writing by obtaining a journalism degree from the University of Montana and later turned to her first love, fiction, to write her grandmother's story.

Heidi's first novel, *Cowgirl Dreams*, has won an EPIC Award and the *USA Book News* Best Book Finalist award. *Follow the Dream*, a WILLA Award winner, is her second book, and *Dare to Dream* is the third in the series about strong, independent Montana women.

Heidi, a member of Women Writing the West and Professional Writers of Prescott, is also a manuscript editor and an avid reader of all kinds of books and enjoys the sunshine and hiking in north-central Arizona, where she writes, edits, and teaches memoir and fiction writing classes.

Married to Dave Thomas (not of Wendy's fame), Heidi is also the "human" for a finicky feline and describes herself primarily as a "cat herder." Visit her at heidimthomas.com.